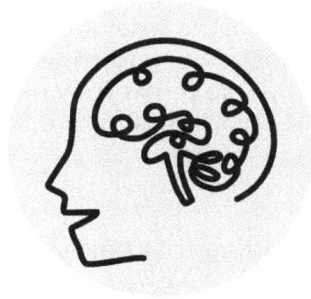

The Adult Speech Therapy
Protocols Pack

An instruction manual for adult speech therapy

Written & Illustrated by
Chung Hwa Brewer, MA, CCC-SLP

Contributors
Miwa Aparo, MOT
Alisha Kleindel, MS, CCC-SLP
Hillary Edwards, MS, CCC-SLP
Tae Sun Krishnek, PT, DPT

FINANCIAL DISCLOSURE:
At the time of publication, the author has a financial relationship with adultspeechtherapy.etsy.com, theadultspeechtherapyworkbook.com, and Medbridge Inc. All other cited or recommended resources have no financial or non-financial relationship with the author.

ISBN: 978-1-7338633-5-3

Also by the author:
The Adult Speech Therapy Workbook (Second Edition, 2024)
The Adult Speech Therapy Workbook (First Edition, 2021)

Cover art and design, page layout, and logo are by the author.

Contents

Hello lovely speech therapy professional,

Thank you for purchasing The Adult Speech Therapy Protocols Pack!

The Protocols Pack is your go-to resource for finding and learning how to do evidence-based treatments for your adult speech therapy patients. It will introduce and guide you through the most common, well-respected, and effective speech therapy treatment options for your patients and, as the name implies, includes step-by-step protocols whenever possible.

This book includes protocols and treatment options for the 12 main areas of adult speech therapy treatment: Dysphagia, Aphasia, AAC, Fluency, Resonance, Voice, Dysarthria, Apraxia, Memory, Attention, Executive Functioning, and Visual Neglect.

We recommend using The Protocols Pack in conjunction with The Adult Speech Therapy Workbook: Second Edition. The Workbook's functional patient worksheets and handouts go hand-in-hand (pun intended) with the instructional information provided in this pack.

To find our other resources, including The Adult Speech Therapy Workbook, visit adultspeechtherapy.co.

With The Protocols Pack in your speech therapy toolkit, we hope that you'll feel more confident on the job and have the space to better enjoy the people you work with everyday!

Ther-happy days,

Chung & The Adult Speech Therapy Team

Dysphagia

Dysphagia

There are many ways to improve swallowing safety, hydration, nutrition, and related quality of life for your patients with dysphagia. You will likely use multiple treatment options to help them reach their goals. When making treatment decisions, consider their preferences, assessment results, physical and cognitive abilities, and available support.

You can use of combination of exercises, compensations and strategies, like maneuver, postural techniques safe swallowing strategies, and environmental and equipment modifications.

Teamwork.

Don't go it alone! If your patient needs support outside your scope of practice, bring in the team.

- Occupational therapy for self-feeding, positioning, and specialized feeding equipment (Brewer, 2023)
- Physical therapy for positioning, strength, and functional mobility
- Nurses and nurse aids for modified medication intake and management of specialized equipment, such as trachs and feeding tubes
- Dietitians to manage hydration and nutrition, including feeding tube management
- Physicians for pharmacological management and referrals for instrumental assessment and diet modifications
- Pharmacists for pharmacological management of GERD, reduced saliva, etc.
- Otolaryngologists for structural or functional issues of the face or neck, including during head and neck cancer treatment
- Respiratory therapists for trach management, breathing or lung conditions, and ventilation or oxygen treatment
- Dentists or prosthodontists for poor oral care, missing teeth, dentures, etc.
- Prosthodontist for making and fitting prosthetics
- Other specialists for procedures like stents, dilation, myotomy, and botox

Instrumental Swallowing Assessments

After completing a bedside swallowing examination, it's best practice to recommend an instrumental swallowing assessment if your patient:

- Demonstrates signs or symptoms of dysphagia and/or aspiration
- Has a history of dysphagia and/or aspiration
- Is at greater risk **not** doing the assessment compared to the minimal risks of the assessment (i.e. radiation exposure)
- Has known or possible structural issues that may impact swallowing (i.e. surgical resection)
- Can follow directions
- Is cooperative and willing
- Is alert
- Is medically stable enough to tolerate the procedure

(Martin-Harris et al., 2021)

If a patient demonstrates signs of dysphagia but doesn't meet these criteria, you can still help them remain safe while eating and drinking. For example, you may work with the nursing team to ensure they are always supervised and helped during meals. You can also introduce modified diets that your patient safely tolerates or start them on simple swallowing exercises

Common Instrumental Swallowing Assessments

The best-known instrumental swallowing assessments are the videofluoroscopic swallowing study (VFSS; also known as the modified barium swallow study), and the fiberoptic endoscopic evaluation of swallowing (FEES).

About videofluoroscopic swallowing studies
The VFSS uses an X-ray to assess the swallow from the oral preparatory to the esophageal phases in real time (Logemann, 1986; American Speech-Language-Hearing Association, n.d.m.) During the procedure, a patient consumes several food and liquid consistencies that are mixed with barium or another contrast material. This substance allows the X-ray to track boluses during a swallow.

VFSS can help you identify when, why, and how laryngeal penetration and/or aspiration occurs. It can also determine which swallowing treatments and compensatory strategies are effective for each patient. A VFSS is usually performed in a hospital's radiology suite by a speech-language pathologist and radiologist.

Patients need to be able to sit upright and travel to the radiology suite for this procedure. The VFSS is contraindicated for patients without a swallow responses or who have a fistula (i.e. tracheoesophageal fistula; American Speech-Language-Hearing Association, n.d.m.)

About fiberoptic endoscopic evaluation of swallowing

The FEES is a procedure that passes a flexible tube through the nose. The tube has a light and camera to watch swallows in real time. It can be performed by a speech-language pathologist, a physician, or both. The FEES can show how safe a patient is with oral intake and which swallowing strategies and therapies are effective. It can also show the vocal cords and how well secretions are being managed (American Speech-Language-Hearing Association, n.d.l.)

With the FEES, there is no radiation exposure and, since it's portable, it can be used in any setting, including at bedside. It's also significantly cheaper to perform than the VFSS.

However, the FEES can't visualize the oral or esophageal phases of swallowing. It can also be more difficult to view than the VFSS, given the camera's movements and the potential of residue getting on the camera.

The FEES is contraindicated for patients with severe movement disorders, agitation, bleeding disorder, or those with trauma to or obstruction of their nasal passage (American Speech-Language-Hearing Association, n.d.l.)

Environmental Modifications

Environmental modifications can improve safety and independence during meals.

All patients who have dysphagia:
- Eat in a quiet environment with minimal background noise (Heape, 2018)
- Have the table clear of everything except what's needed for the meal
- Have enough lighting
- Choose a comfortable seat that supports good posture
- Choose a feeding time when they're not fatigued
- Use adaptive equipment when needed
- Avoid multitasking

Patients who also have cognitive impairments:
- Have only one food item on the table at a time
- Avoid glare, such as shiny or reflective tables, placemats, or menus
- Use solid-colored dishes and table coverings with no patterns
- Add visual contrast, such as a light-colored placemat on a dark table
- If you can't avoid a noisy environment, move to a quieter table or add white noise
- Display their safe swallowing strategies, such as a laminated or framed list
- Add self-feeding or hand-over-hand to increase sensory input
(Mansolillo, n.d.a.; American Speech-Language-Hearing Association, n.d.d.)

Patients who also have physical impairments:
- Be mindful of fatigue. Adjust seating, food textures, utensils, and caloric density. Organize the space to conserve energy (Tabor et al., 2017)
- If a patient has unilateral physical or visuospatial impairment, put food and drink on the unaffected side

Diet and Liquid Modifications

The purpose of diet texture modifications is to increase swallowing safety and efficiency. You may modify a diet to decrease the time and effort required to consume a meal in order to support nutrition and hydration. Or you may modify textures to avoid choking, aspiration, and/or pneumonia (Yang et al., 2023).

Diet modifications include:
- Pureed (IDDSI Level 4)
- Minced and Moist (IDDSI Level 5)
- Soft and Bite-Sized (IDDSI Level 6)
- Easy to Chew (IDDSI Level 7)

Liquid modifications include:
- Thin liquids (IDDSI Level 0)
- Slightly thick (IDDSI Level 1)
- Mildly thick (IDDSI Level 2)
- Moderately thick (IDDSI Level 3)
- Extremely thick (IDDSI Level 4)

See the International Dysphagia Diet Standardisation Initiative (IDDSI) for more information.

More About Thickened Liquids

Thickened liquids slow down the bolus. Increasing the thickness of liquids can decrease the rate of aspiration (although not necessarily the risk of aspiration pneumonia, Yang et al., 2023). Thickened liquids can also cause physiological changes like increased pharyngeal pressure and UES relaxation.

When patients are on thickened liquids, they are at an increased risk of dehydration, which can have its own side effects (urinary tract infections, impaired cognition, increased falls; Robbins et al., 2008; Werden Abrams et al., 2023). Dehydration likely occurs because thickened liquids are less appetizing than thin liquids. The Frazier Water Protocol can help reduce the risk of dehydration, so consider it for patients you believe would benefit from thickened liquids (Werden Abrams et al., 2023).

Trial thickened liquids with your patient during an instrumental swallowing assessment to see how they respond to them. Make your recommendations from there.

A modified diet may also increase the risk of dehydration, even more so than thickened liquids. Talk to a registered dietitian about your plan of care and get their feedback.

Other general advice about diet and liquid modifications

Before modifying a diet, consider risk factors, cognition, motivation, buy-in, and care partner support. Everyone aspirates from time to time. Moreover, even if a patient aspirates, it doesn't automatically lead to pneumonia. Consider the least restrictive and safest diet for your patient. Continue to monitor their intake and safety and upgrade diets as needed.

If you do recommend changes, review your patient's recommended diet with them, including specific foods they should or shouldn't eat. Identify foods your patient enjoys eating and help them create a meal plan. Offer tips for preparing foods that fit their diet and needs. For example, you may recommend a small food processor or personal blender for patients who want to save money and counter space.

You can also alter foods as a form of sensory stimulation for people who require more (or less) sensory input. For example, you may alternate hot and cold items, give thermal tactile stimulation, adjust for tactile defensiveness, or otherwise increase sensation (sour flavors, carbonation, minty flavors, capsaicin, etc; Ebihara et al., 2006; Wang et al., 2019).

Frazier Water Protocol

This protocol helps certain patients who aspirate on thin liquids to drink water without increasing their risk of aspiration pneumonia (Gillman et al., 2017). The Frazier Water Protocol posits that because our bodies are made up of water (which has a neutral pH with little bacteria), our lung mucosal tissue can absorb small amounts of clean, aspirated water without harm. The protocol was named after Frazier Rehabilitation Hospital, where it was developed.

Before recommending the Frazier Water Protocol, complete a swallowing assessment, an instrumental swallowing assessment, and the Oral Health Assessment Tool.

Patients who demonstrate ANY of the following should NOT use this protocol:
- Can't remain awake and alert while drinking
- Are impulsive or have severe cognitive impairments
- Have a degenerative neurological dysfunction
- Have an absent pharyngeal swallow response (per instrumental swallowing assessment)
- Can't consistently get out of bed
- Can't maintain an upright posture while drinking
- Experience excessive discomfort, coughing, or choking when drinking
- Have current or suspected aspiration pneumonia or acute pulmonary issues
- Have thrush or oral bacterial infection
- Are dependent without care partners to provide good oral care

The Frazier Water Protocol patient instructions
- Brush your teeth and tongue 2-3 times daily or as instructed by your speech therapist
- When eating, do not drink un-thickened water. Only drink thickened water while eating
- Wait 30 minutes after eating before drinking un-thickened water
- Water is given only when you ask for it and in a small amount (one cup or teaspoon of water at a time, not a large bottle)
- Do not take medications with water
- Use swallowing strategies as needed while drinking un-thickened water

Ice Chip Protocol

Patients with severe dysphagia who are likely to aspirate on any kind of bolus may benefit from the Ice Chip Protocol. According to the protocol's creators, any patient receiving tube feedings is a good candidate.

Like the Frazier Water Protocol, the premise of the Ice Chip Protocol is that aspirating small amounts of clean water is not inherently harmful. Eating ice chips can also significantly benefit patients by increasing swallowing frequency.

Ice chips should be about the size of a pea. Before recommending the Ice Chip Protocol, complete an instrumental assessment to observe oral control and movement, initiation of swallowing, airway closure, penetration or aspiration, secretion management, pharyngeal clearance, and the patient's response (Pisegna & Langmore, 2018).

Signs that your patient may be ready for this protocol include:
- Good oral control
- No or minimal spillage
- Spontaneous throat clear or cough clears any aspirates
- Manageable secretions (if applicable)
- Would benefit from increased frequency of swallowing
- Alert
- Can sit upright
- Performs good oral care at least 2 times every day

Ice Chip Protocol (Pisegna & Langmore, 2018)
- Complete thorough oral care immediately before the protocol.
- Place ice chips on a clean spoon (equaling less than 2 ml fluid water, to start).
- Ask your patient to move the ice chips around in their mouth and swallow all at once when they're ready.
- Complete 3 trials. It may take several attempts to fully engage the swallow, especially for patients on NPO. Observe oral control, secretions, vitals, and the patient's response.
- If safe, continue offering ice chips by spoon.
- Stop if you suspect no swallow initiation or observe excess anterior spillage or signs of aspiration.

Oral Sensory Stimulation

An underlying sensory issue may worsen or even cause dysphagia. This is because our bodies rely on sensory feedback to time each stage of the swallow. For some patients, the sensory input of regular food and liquids is no longer strong enough to alert their brains to begin the next stage. Here's where speech therapy comes in.

If your patient demonstrates bolus holding or prolonged mastication, they may need stronger oral stimulation to help progress with the feeding, with chewing, or with initiating the swallow.

Try carbonation, sour items, or hot or cold items.
- Add oral stimulation during therapy (e.g. lemon glycerin swabs to induce swallows)
- Or, add in oral stimulation during meals (e.g. alternate between hot and cold items to encourage mastication)
- Test sensory stimuli to see what your patient responds to

People who have Parkinson's Disease may benefit from added flavors (honey, salt) or alternating between sweet and salty (Mansolillo, n.d.c.) Be sure to adhere to any dietary restrictions.

The goal is for your patients, especially those with non-progressive conditions, to chew and swallow in a more timely manner. The ultimate goal is for their brains to rewire enough to eat a more normal diet (not just sour, carbonated food or drink!)

Respiratory Muscle Strength Training

Expiratory Muscle Strength Training (EMST)

EMST strengthens the expiratory and submental muscles needed to breathe out forcefully, swallow, and cough. Patients blow forcefully into a handheld device until they reach a specified pressure threshold. They follow an exercise protocol to increase their strength over time. EMST may improve suprahyoid movement and penetration-aspiration scale scores (Park et al., 2016).

Inspiratory Muscle Strength Training (IMST)

IMST strengthens and improves the endurance of the diaphragm, inspiratory muscles, and some upper airway muscles. Patients inhale fast and forcefully into a handheld device until they reach a specified threshold. IMST can improve swallowing safety and intake levels (Liaw et al., 2020).

Populations that may benefit from EMST and/or IMST

- Dysphagia due to weak cough
- Reduced airway protection
- Stroke
- Traumatic brain injury
- Head and neck cancer
- COPD (chronic obstructive pulmonary disease)
- Parkinson's disease (Troche 2010; Winiker and Kertscher 2023)
- ALS (amyotrophic lateral sclerosis), for **some** patients early in the ALS disease progression.
    - The research recommends respiratory muscle strength training for patients with ALS who have normal or mildly impaired lung function, a neurology consult before starting the treatment, and a device calibrated to 30% to 50% of their max pressure (Richardson, n.d.; Plowman, 2019; Robison, 2018).
- MS (multiple sclerosis)
    - IMST may improve respiratory strength and dyspnea in patients with MS (Martin-Sanchez et al., 2020). EMST may improve airway protection, cough, and saliva management (Silverman et al., 2017; Gosselink et al., 2000). It's essential to focus on energy conservation and never push a patient with MS to the point of fatigue.

- Dysarthria
- Myasthenia gravis
- Guillain-Barre syndrome

Get physician approval and proceed with caution if a patient has:
- Uncontrolled hypertension
- Untreated GERD
- VP shunt
- Current multiple-sclerosis flare or myasthenia gravis crisis
- Asthma
- Or is pregnant

Contraindications for EMST and IMST include
- Stroke or neurosurgery that happened immediately before starting EMST or IMST
- Breathing problems unrelated to respiratory weakness
- Patients with whom the Valsalva maneuver is contraindicated
- History of spontaneous pneumothorax or traumatic pneumothorax
- Unhealed rib fractures
- Had a tympanic membrane rupture/myringotomy/other perforation within 30 days
- Abdominal hernia or recent abdominal surgery

(National Foundation of Swallowing Disorders, 2021; Aspire Products LLC, n.d.)

Swallowing Exercises: General Advice

Swallowing exercises aim to increase muscle strength, speed, range of motion, and/or swallow coordination. They treat an underlying physiological impairment to improve function. Swallowing exercises can lead to meaningful change, such as improved penetration-aspiration scores and reduced signs and symptoms of aspiration.

Use exercises with alert patients who can follow directions and have an underlying physiological impairment, such as muscle weakness.

Popular Evidence-Based Swallowing Exercises

- Effortful swallow (Bahia & Lowell, 2020; Yang et al., 2023; Kim & Kim, 2023)
- Mendelsohn maneuver (Yang et al., 2023)
- Respiratory muscle strength training (Park et al., 2016; Liaw et al., 2020)
- Tongue hold (American Speech-Language-Hearing Association, n.d.d.)
- Effortful pitch glide (Miloro et al., 2014)
- Head lift exercise (American Speech-Language-Hearing Association, n.d.d.)
- Chin tuck against resistance (Yang et al., 2023; Park and Hwang, 2021)
- Jaw opening exercise (Koyama et al., 2017)
- Straw suck
- Lips exercises (Hägglund et al., 2017)
- Tongue exercises and stretches (Robbins et al., 2007, Kim et al., 2017; Hwang et al., 2019)

Choosing Exercises and Strategies

Although dysphagia exercise research may sometimes be inconclusive or contradictory (e.g. the Mendelsohn maneuver improved range of motion in one study but not another), don't despair! Dysphagia interventions work.

While the research may not always spell out exactly what to do with each patient, this section offers plenty of evidence-based exercises and strategies to choose from.

It's best to trial most swallowing exercises and strategies during an instrumental assessment. This allows you to see if the move is making the impact you hope it will on your patient's swallowing.

Some exercises, like the Mendelsohn Maneuver, have extensive evidence supporting them but are hard to do. They may be especially hard for patients with severe pain, apraxia of speech, or more severe cognitive impairments. That said, the potential benefits of these exercises may outweigh a long learning curve. Try them with your patients if they're motivated, will make progress, and you believe it's best for them.

Principles of Exercise and Neuroplasticity

Understanding how exercise works can help you make better dysphagia treatment choices. You can read more about the principles of neuroplasticity and motor learning in the Appendix.

Prep the patient. Set your patient up for success before assigning an exercise. Take the time to make sure that your patients are:
- Motivated. Dysphagia exercises are tough. Being motivated can help your patient stay focused on their goals.
- Understand the expectations. Ensure they know how to do the exercises correctly and why.
- Stimulable for the exercise you choose. Test to see whether they can do the movement, respond to certain cues, etc.

Emphasize the correct form. Take the time to teach the correct form. Strengthening bad form is counterproductive. Take a break if your patient's form starts to slip at any time.

Dosage and intensity. Intensity matters. Push the system beyond everyday use to make changes.

When deciding how hard to push their system, balance your patient's pain, fatigue, and other factors. Ask questions and modify the plan as needed to keep your treatment safe and effective.

As your patient improves, gradually make the exercise more challenging. You may do this by increasing the number of repetitions, speed, how long they hold a move, or the size and complexity of the bolus.

There is no ideal dosage, so you can be flexible based on what your patient needs. Here are general recommendations for dysphagia exercises:

- **Number of repetitions**
  The number of repetitions will depend on the exercise and on your patient. In general:
    - To increase strength and neuromuscular facilitation, do 8-12 repetitions per set of an exercise.
    - Do 3-4 sets per day, 3-5 times per week.
    - Or, they may hold a static exercise for gradually longer periods of time. An example is working up to hold the head lift exercise for 1 minute.
    - Increase the difficulty once they become consistent with the exercise and can maintain proper form without cues.
    - Repeat until the point of fatigue, as appropriate.

- **Resistance and effort**
    - Increase the difficulty once they are consistent with the exercise and can maintain proper form without cues. For example, introduce heavier boluses, provide more resistance during lingual exercises, etc.

- **Duration**
    - An exercise program of 8-10 weeks is typical in exercise science. Some patients may need a longer duration.

Patient factors. Consider age, diagnoses, and overall physical functioning when designing an exercise program. For example, expiratory muscle strength training is recommended for some with multiple sclerosis and ALS, but only with diagnosis-specific modifications (Silverman et al., 2017; Gosselink et al., 2000; Plowman et al., 2019).

Specificity matters. The best exercise for swallowing is swallowing! This means that if your patient can elicit a swallow, do swallowing exercises (vs other laryngeal exercises).

That being said, some patients may find swallowing too challenging, fatiguing, or frustrating. In that case, get transference on your side:

Transference is a sign of neuroplasticity. It occurs when one training experience transfers to or enhances a related skill. While the goal of exercise may not be to elicit transference, we add it here as a reminder that it can happen! For example, some oral-motor exercises can improve chewing and swallowing abilities. Other examples of transference are talking loud (LSVT LOUD®), exhalation exercises (EMST), and head lifts (Shaker exercise). These treatments can all improve swallowing even though the patient doesn't swallow as part of the exercise.

Dysphagia Exercise Protocols

Here are patient instructions for evidence-based dysphagia exercises, maneuvers, and stretches.

Super-Supraglottic Swallow Maneuver
1. Take a deep breath and hold it tight.
2. Take a bite/sip while holding your breath.
3. Swallow hard.
4. Cough right after swallowing.
5. Take a breath.

Effortful Swallow Exercise/Maneuver
Swallow us ng _____ (e.g., saliva, water).
1. Swallow as hard as you can. Pretend that you're swallowing a whole grape.
2. Relax and repeat.

Mendelsohn Maneuver
1. Gently place your fingers on the front of your throat.
2. Swallow your saliva and feel your larynx move up and down.
3. Swallow your saliva again, but this time hold up your larynx at its highest point during the swallow.
4. Hold for up to 3 seconds.
5. Relax and repeat.

Head Lift Exercise
1. Lie flat on your back. Don't use a pillow.
2. Raise your head to look at your toes, holding your head up for 60 seconds. Keep your shoulders on the ground and breathe through your nose.
3. Relax back down for 60 seconds.
4. Repeat.

Tongue Press Up Exercise
1. Lift your tongue and press your whole tongue hard against the roof of your mouth.
2. Hold for 10 seconds.
3. Relax for 10 seconds.
4. Repeat.

Chin Tuck Against Resistance Exercise
1. Sit upright, then lightly press a rolled-up hand towel under your chin and against your neck (you can also use a squishy ball or your fist).
2. Press your chin down into the towel and hold for 60 seconds. Relax for 60 seconds.
3. Repeat step 2.
4. Press your chin down into the towel and hold for 3 seconds. Relax for 3 seconds.
5. Repeat step 4.

Jaw Opening Exercise
1. Lightly place the tip of your tongue against the roof of your mouth.
2. Place your fist under your chin and press up.
3. Slowly open your jaw. Continue pressing up with your fist.
4. Relax and repeat.

Effortful Pitch Glide Exercise
1. Glide on the 'eee' sound from a low pitch to a high pitch. Squeeze the muscles in your throat.
2. Hold the highest pitch possible for 3-5 seconds.
3. Relax and repeat.

Straw Suck Exercise
1. Place a straw into a thickened liquid.
2. Place your lips around the straw and suck continuously for 3 seconds or until the liquid reaches your mouth.
3. When the liquid reaches your mouth, swallow HARD.
4. Relax and repeat.

Lip Exercises
1. Sit upright, preferably with a backrest.
2. Place an oral ring or tongue depressor between your lips.
3. Tighten your lips and resist as the clinician pulls on the device for 5-10 seconds.
4. Rest and repeat.

Tongue Press Up Exercise
1. Lift your tongue up and press your whole tongue hard against the roof of your mouth.
2. Hold for 10 seconds.
3. Relax for 10 seconds.
4. Repeat.

Tongue Pull Back Exercise
1. Stick your tongue out. The speech therapist will hold your tongue using clean, gloved fingers.
2. Pull your tongue to the back of your throat. Your speech therapist will gently hold your tongue to provide resistance.
3. Relax and repeat.

Tongue Out
1. Stick your tongue out as far as you can.
2. Hold for 5 seconds.
3. Relax and repeat.

Tongue Back
1. Retract your tongue as far back as you can.
2. Hold for 5 seconds.
3. Relax and repeat.

Tongue Out-Then-Back
1. Protrude your tongue out, then retract it back in.
2. Hold each for 5 seconds.
3. 3. Relax and repeat.

Tongue Right
1. Stick your tongue out as far to the right as you can.
2. Hold for 5 seconds.
3. Relax and repeat.

Tongue Left
1. Stick your tongue out as far to the left as you can.
2. Hold for 5 seconds.
3. Relax and repeat.

Tongue Up
1. Lift your tongue up as far as you can (like you're trying to lick your nose).
2. Hold it for a count of 5 seconds
3. Relax and repeat.

Tongue Down
1. Stick your tongue down as far as you can (like you're trying to lick your chin).
2. Hold for 5 seconds.
3. Relax and repeat.

Tongue Around (Out)

1. Stick out your tongue and lick all around your lip in one direction (clockwise). Relax.
2. Then, go around in the other direction (counter-clockwise). Relax.
3. Repeat in each direction.

Tongue Around (In)

1. Move the tongue clockwise inside your mouth. Relax.
2. Move your tongue around in the other direction. Relax.
3. Repeat in each direction.

Dysphagia Exercise Devices

Exercise devices can enhance dysphagia treatment for some patients. They can cost anywhere from around $50 per patient to over $3,000 for a shared device. Hopefully, your workplace is willing to invest in the speech therapy department. If not, you may need to advocate for your patients (and field!) Start by reviewing the literature with your employer.

Tongue pressure manometers
Measure tongue and lip strength with a tongue pressure manometer such as the IOPI®. This device typically features an air-filled bulb on one end and a hand-held measurement device on the other. The manometer provides visual biofeedback in the form of a row of lights. Using a manometer can improve tongue and suprahyoid functioning. It can be purchased or rented.

Surface electromyography
sEMG uses electrodes placed on the skin of the lower face and neck to measure muscle activity. It provides visual feedback via a row of lights on a graph on a computer screen. sEMG can be helpful for training in the Mendelsohn maneuver, effortful swallow, or jaw opening exercise. There are several sEMG devices to choose from, including the Pathway® MR series.

Respiratory Muscle Strength Training (EMST & IMST)
Expiratory muscle strength training (EMST) can improve suprahyoid movement and penetration-aspiration scores by strengthening expiratory and submental muscles (Park et al., 2016). Patients blow strong and fast into a device (such as the EMST150™) until they reach a certain pressure threshold. Inspiratory muscle strength training (IMST) strengthens and improves the endurance of the diaphragm, inspiratory muscles, and some upper airway muscles (Liaw et al., 2020). Patients inhale fast and forcefully into a handheld device (such the POWER®Breathe IMT) until they reach a specified threshold.

Neuromuscular electrical stimulation (NMES)
NMES devices, like Ampcare and VitalStim® (Yang et al., 2023), deliver small electrical currents via electrodes placed on the skin of the face or neck. These currents cause muscles to contract. This stimulation can improve airway closure and overall swallowing safety when used during a swallow.

TheraBite Jaw Motion Rehab System

This device is for patients with trismus. Trismus is limited mouth opening due to muscle tightness, usually caused by cancer treatment, burns, or a stroke. To use this device, the patient inserts a mouthpiece with a lever that slowly opens, stretching the jaw.

If you or your patient are unable to purchase the device, you can make a similar one using tongue depressors and tape (look up the ARK-J Stretching Device).

Aspiration Risk Factors

Your patient may be at a higher risk of aspiration if they have any of the following:

- Poor oral hygiene
- Minimal or poor dentition
- Reduced salvia
- Dysphonia
- Dysarthria
- Abnormal or weak cough
- Need help with feeding or oral care
- Resist feeding
- History of smoking
- Neck trauma
- History of tracheostomy
- Feeling full very quickly

- Unintentional weight loss
- Dehydration
- Poor positioning
- Take extra effort and time to complete meals
- History of respiratory infections and pneumonia
- Take multiple swallows with every bite or sip
- Acid reflux
- Tongue pumping
- Impulsive eating behaviors
- Impaired cognition

What Diet Level to Start On

Your patient's first modified diet is often the textures and liquids they can safely consume in 80%+ of opportunities when using strategies.

Your patient should be able to stay alert throughout the food and liquid trials. Complete oral care before the trials.

Complete Food and Liquid Trials

1. **PLOF liquid: small amounts.** Trial small amounts of their previous level of functioning (PLOF) liquids. For example, a teaspoon of thin liquids.

2. **PLOF liquid: larger amounts.** If they tolerate small amounts well, trial larger amounts. For example, cup sips of thin liquids.

3. **Add strategies.** If they demonstrate signs or symptoms of dysphagia, introduce strategies and trial small amounts again. For example, teaspoons of thin liquids with cues to bolus hold.

4. **Dysphagia goal.** If your patient safely consumes in 80-100% of trials with strategies, your dysphagia goal could be to continue trials with speech therapy using those strategies (as needed) at that diet level. For example, "Recommend continued teaspoon sips of thin liquids given bolus hold with speech therapy only."

5. **PLOF food: small amount.** Trial small amounts of the PLOF diet textures. For example, a teaspoon of regular textures.

6. **PLOF food: larger amount.** If the patient tolerates small amounts well, trial larger amounts. For example, bites of regular textures.

7. **Add strategies.** If they demonstrate signs or symptoms of dysphagia, introduce strategies and trial small amounts again. For example, teaspoons of regular textures with prompts to swallow.

8. **Dysphagia goal.** If your patient safely consumes in 80-100% of trials with strategies, your dysphagia goal could be to continue trials in speech therapy using those strategies (as needed) at that diet level. For example, "Recommend continued regular texture diet with cues for small bites and sips with speech therapy only."

9. **Softer foods.** If your patient still demonstrates signs/symptoms of dysphagia given strategies, trial softer foods. Trial thicker liquids during an instrumental assessment.

10. **Get to 80%.** Continue to use strategies and introduce progressively softer foods until your patient can safely swallow in about 80% of trials. Do the same with thicker liquids during an instrumental assessment.

Alternate Nutrition and Hydration: Tube Feedings

With patients who have feeding tubes, you'll often work towards eating and drinking by mouth. This is because most feeding tubes are temporary, and you're preparing the patient to get nutrition/hydration by mouth again.

Types of Feeding Tubes

Enteral feeding tubes deliver food, liquid, or medications straight to the stomach or small intestine. The tube may be placed in the mouth (orogastric or 'OG'), nose (nasogastric or 'NG'), stomach (PEG), or small intestine (PEJ). An enteral feeding tube is often recommended because of severe dysphagia, gastrointestinal issues, or injuries or surgeries that make chewing or swallowing difficult. OG and NG tubes remain in place for 2-4 weeks. PEG and PEJ tubes are surgically placed for longer-term use.

Parenteral nutrition is delivered directly into the vein. This option bypasses the digestive system ("para" means "pass by"). This option is often used when the digestive system can't tolerate or absorb nutrition or if there are other serious gastrointestinal issues. Patients may receive this type of nutrition partially (PPN) or totally (TPN).

Enteral and parenteral tubes are connected to feeding pouches filled with formula/nutrition. Physicians and dietitians determine the patient's feeding schedule. Patients may be on gravity drip feedings, where the pouch slowly empties over time. Or they may be on pump feedings, where the pouch empties throughout the day (continuous feedings) or during set meal times (bolus feeding).

Dysphagia Treatment and Tube Feedings

Most feeding tubes are temporary. If that's the case for your patient, help their chewing and swallowing skills be ready for nutrition by mouth by doing food or liquid trials. Check with their physician, surgeon, and dietitian before starting trials. Start with ice chips or small amounts of water and work toward larger boluses and/or different textures.

NPO Diets

While surgeons, gastroenterologists, and other providers may place patients on NPO diets for other reasons, speech therapy typically reserves NPO diets for patients who:
- Have no swallowing reflex
- Have no UES opening
- Demonstrated severe dysphagia during a bedside swallow examination and are waiting for an instrumental assessment

Working with patients who are on NPO
Seeing "NPO" in a new patient's chart can be intimidating. If you don't yet have the skills to manage a patient who is NPO, get training by shadowing a more experienced speech-language pathologist and otherwise getting educated. Some programs, like the McNeill Dysphagia Therapy Program, can be used with patients who are NPO. Some also include great information about the swallowing mechanism.

As you wait for the results of an instrumental assessment, you can still work on the following:
- Intensive oral care (Watando et al., 2004)
- Frazier Water Protocol
- Ice chips protocol
- Secretion management
- Some swallowing exercises
- Volitional cough
- Directed cough (Novaleski et al., 2024)
- Incentive spirometry
- Improving breath support

Communicate with the care team
Keep in touch with your patient's physician, dietitian, gastroenterologist, and/or respiratory therapist. Get medical clearance to begin food and liquid trials and update the team on their progress.

Complete food and liquid trials
Getting patients off an NPO diet is a very similar process to advancing a modified diet. Patients can greatly benefit from intensive oral care, an ice-chips protocol, and the Frazier Water Protocol. Monitor your patient's vitals, fatigue level, and lung sounds closely. The nursing team can help monitor your patient between your visits.

Head and Neck Cancer

Speech therapy for patients with head and neck cancer (HNC) aims to minimize the side effects of cancer and cancer treatment and improve swallowing function throughout the cancer journey (American Speech-Language-Hearing Association, n.d.i.)

Goals for HNC patients

The goal of speech therapy changes depending on where your patient is on their head and neck cancer journey (Messing et al., 2017). Before surgery, chemotherapy, or radiation, educate patients about what changes to expect in their chewing and swallowing. You may also introduce safe swallowing strategies, stretches, and exercises to reduce impairment, maintain function, and improve recovery.

During and after cancer treatment, you'll modify exercises, stretches, compensations, and diets to meet their needs. In general:

Before cancer treatment:
- Teach exercises to maintain muscle strength and range of motion (e.g., jaw and tongue range of motion exercises, effortful swallow)
- Educate on how to maintain adequate hydration and nutrition via mouth
- Educate about swallowing function and safety

During cancer treatment:
- Continue swallowing exercises and stretches as tolerated
- Maximize oral intake as tolerated
- Manage xerostomia and other side effects
- Complete tracheostomy care, if needed

After cancer treatment:
- Restore strength and range of motion (e.g., jaw and tongue range of motion exercises, effortful swallow)
- Restore swallowing skills impacted by cancer treatment
- Recommend oral prostheses to compensate for resections, if needed

Trachs: Cuff Deflation Trials

Your patient's tracheostomy tube may have an inflated cuff. The cuff blocks air from going toward the nose and mouth so that it can flow through the trach instead. For your patient to be able to speak, the cuff must be deflated so that air can pass over their vocal folds once again. Only start cuff-deflation trials if it has cleared by their physician and/or respiratory therapist AND you're appropriately trained.

If you're not proficient at working with tracheostomies, ask your employer for training. They may have you shadow an experienced speech-language pathologist or nurse and/or complete a training course. There are also free online webinars and courses on trach care, like those from Passy Muir®. MedBridge also has excellent training courses (with a paid subscription).

Prep your patient
Cuff deflation can make breathing feel different, which can be uncomfortable or scary for patients. Communicate clearly and often to help them understand what's happening during each step of the cuff deflation trials.

Don't rush. Take things one step at a time and explain what you're doing. Make time for their questions, explain what to expect next, and get consent before proceeding. Involve loved ones so that the focus can be on the joy of communicating (Kobak, n.d.)

Begin cuff deflation trials:

1. Wash and dry your hands and don personal protective equipment (gloves, mask, etc.)

2. Clean the trach. Learn how on the U.S. Department of Veterans Affairs guide to Cleaning Your Tracheostomy Inner Cannula and Skin.

3. Wash and dry your hands and put on a clean pair of gloves.

4. Make sure your patient's airway is clear (zero secretions) and suction as needed.

5. Deflate the cuff. Use a clean 10 CC syringe to slowly remove the air from the pilot balloon, about 2 CCs at a time.
   o Provide breaks and suctioning as needed.
   o Continue removing air until the pilot balloon is just empty of air. Lightly pinch the pouch to ensure it's flat and not bouncy.
   o Record how many CCs of air you removed. After the trial, you will re-insert the same amount to re-inflate the cuff.

6. Time how long your patient tolerates cuff deflation.
   o The parameters for "good" tolerance vary from setting to setting.
   o Signs of poor tolerance include a change in vitals, looking distressed, and/or difficulty breathing (Barnes, n.d.)

7. Complete speech trials and speaking valve trials when your patient is ready for them. This will be determined by your work setting's protocols.

8. After the trials, reinflate the cuff with the same amount of air that you removed.

9. Continue monitoring your patient's vitals. Leave the room only after their vitals are within normal limits and stable for at least a few minutes.

10. Communicate with your patient, their nurse, physician, and/or respiratory therapist about how your patient tolerated the cuff deflation trial.

Trachs: Speech Trials With Cuff Deflation

Once your patient tolerates cuff deflation, the next logical step is speech trials! However, only attempt speech trials if you've been appropriately trained. If you need training, speak with your facility.

Your patient may be appropriate for speech trials with cuff deflation if they meet **ALL** of the following requirements:
- Alert and able to follow commands
- Meet the criteria set by the speaking valve manufacturer
- Safely tolerated cuff deflations. This typically means oxygen saturation, heart rate, and respiratory rate are stable and within normal limits (check with your setting for specific parameters)
- Are medically stable
- Cleared by their physician and/or respiratory therapist to do so
- Can manage their secretions

Contraindications for a speaking valve include patients with:
- Severe upper airway obstruction
- High aspiration risk
- Excessive secretions they can't manage
- Impaired cognition
- Inability to tolerate cuff deflation
- Severe medical fragility and/or medical instability (Bier et al., 2004)

The cuff must be DEFLATED before placing a one-way speaking valve.

Prepping your patient:
Communicate often with your patient throughout the trial. Speaking valve trials can feel scary or uncomfortable, so explain what you're going to do before you do it so your patient understands what is happening. Make time for their questions via writing, texting, or other AAC. Involve loved ones so the focus can be on the joy of communicating (Kobak, n.d.)

Begin speaking trials:

1. Wash and dry your hands and don personal protective equipment (gloves, mask, etc.) before touching the trach.
2. Monitor your patient's vitals throughout the trial.
3. Deflate the tracheostomy cuff, following the instructions above in Trachs: Cuff Deflation Trials.
4. Begin speech trials with digital occlusion. Prepare your patient before starting.
   - For example: "Let's do a practice run. I'm going to ask you to say, 'Ahhhh.' As soon as you breathe out, I'm going to place my finger here so you can speak. Let's try this one time."
5. Cover the entire trach using a gloved finger (SLP-provided digital occlusion) **only** when your patient breathes out.
6. Immediately remove your finger as soon as the exhale is complete so your patient can inhale.
   - Your patient will typically need at least a few trials before they produce any voice. Give breaks as needed and continue to monitor their vitals. Be encouraging!
7. Once the patient can consistently say "ahhh," ask them to say other vowel sounds, such as "hello" and their first name.
8. Once the patient feels comfortable with speaking, they may provide the digital occlusion (patient-provided digital occlusion). Make sure they are using a clean, gloved finger. They may say vowel sounds, cough, or clear their throat.
9. Gradually work up to several minutes of cuff deflation with speech trials. Ask yes/no questions, then simple open-ended questions. Work up to simple conversation while monitoring their vitals and fatigue level. Stop as needed.
10. Re-inflate the cuff when the speech trials are done.

Share updates on how speech trials are going with your patient's nurse, physician, and/or respiratory therapist at least weekly. Discuss your recommendations and whether it's medically safe to continue your plan.

Train the patient/care partner on how to deflate and re-inflate the cuff correctly, as needed. Encourage your patient to use a pulse oximeter throughout the day to monitor their own oxygen saturation levels.

Trachs: Speaking Valve Trials

Speaking valves, like the popular Passy Muir® valve (PMV), can be used instead of digital occlusion for patients who can tolerate it. Your patient may be a candidate for a PMV if they tolerate cuff deflation and can phonate with digital occlusion—see the PMV website for a Readiness Assessment and Use protocol.

Never use a speaking valve with a foam-filled cuffed trach tube. Always deflate the trach cuff before placing a speaking valve.

Ensure the valve is clean before placing it: Clean it using warm, soapy water, rinse it thoroughly, and allow it to air dry.

Again, monitor your patient's vitals throughout speaking valve trials. Remove the valve immediately if your patient has difficulty breathing. Provide breaks, suctioning, and oxygen as needed.

Before placing a PMV:
- Position your patient in a comfortable, upright posture.
- Wash and dry your hands.
- Put on personal protective equipment (gloves, mask, eye protection, etc.)
- Clear the patient's airway of secretions.
- Suction the trach and mouth and ask your patient to blow their nose, as needed.
- Deflate the trach cuff. Continue to monitor vitals and breathing. Suction and provide breaks and oxygen as needed.

How to place a PMV:
- Hold the neck plate (flange) in place with one hand to avoid twisting the trach.
- Place the speaking valve. If you use a Passy Muir Valve, place it on the tracheostomy tube opening and give a gentle, one-quarter turn to the right (clockwise).
    - Encourage your patient to cough. Provide oral suction as needed.
- Observe your patient closely for signs of distress, such as increased heart rate, discomfort, or work of breath. Reinflate the cuff and/or provide oxygen as needed.

Speech trials with a PMV:

- Encourage your patient to vocalize.
  - You may need to start with sustained phonation souncs, such as "ahhh," then work up to words and beyond.
- Check their swallowing abilities with the speaking valve in place, if indicated.
- Gradually increase the speaking valve wear time. Start with short intervals and gradually extend the time.

After speech trials with a PMV:

- Reinflate the cuff and provide suction as needed
- Assess vitals and breathing.
- Clean the speaking valve with warm water and a few drops cf mild, fragrance-free dish liquid.
  - **Don't** use peroxide, bleach, vinegar, alcohol, brushes, or cotton swabs to clean the speaking valve.
  - Air dry only.
- Appropriately clean other equipment, complete hand hygiene, and provide patient education.

Share updates on how speech trials are going with your patient's nurse, physician, and/or respiratory therapist at least weekly. Discuss your recommendations and whether it's medically safe to continue your plan. For example, discuss using a speaking valve between therapy sess ons or longer periods of cuff deflation.

Train the patient/care partner on how to deflate and re-inflate the cuff correctly, as needed. Encourage your patient to use a pulse oximeter throughout the day to monitor their own oxygen saturation levels.

Aphasia

Aphasia

Unlike many other areas of speech therapy, aphasia has many treatment approaches and protocols. A protocol can be helpful because it lays out each step and how to cue. That said, you don't need a protocol to improve language. These aphasia treatments typically still include a prompt (picture card, written word), strategy, and cue. Both are included in this guide.

Language Expression and Writing Exercises

Naming therapy can improve expressive language, especially when written prompts are added (Sze et al., 2020).

How to make naming therapy easier. To make naming easier, have patients name the opposite word or the other part of a pair. These are easier because there are fewer words to choose from. Plus, the words are already associated in the patient's mind. For example, it's easier for your patient to name the opposite of "right" than if you pointed and asked what direction you're pointing. Naming half of an obvious pair is also easier. For example, "What goes with salt?" is easier to name than if you described "pepper" and asked them to name it.

How to make naming therapy harder. If your patient needs more of a challenge, use abstract targets and ask open-ended questions. For example, "love" and "pain" (abstract words) are harder to name than something concrete like "chair" or "boat." And "What is this?" (open-ended prompt) is harder to name than a closed-ended prompt, such as "What is something you read?"

Language Comprehension and Reading Exercises

Offer encouragement, take breaks as needed, and continue to build rapport.

Many language comprehension and reading exercises require working memory. If your patient has a memory impairment, work on their strongest language modality (reading or listening) first to make the tasks easier and set them up for success.

How to help patients answer yes/no questions and follow directions:
- **Repeat the question while emphasizing keywords** ("Is it nighttime?" using a confused tone)
- **Give verbal cues** ("The sun is up, and it's almost lunchtime")
- **Gesture** with the target body part (wiggle your shoulders as you say, "Shrug your shoulders")
- **Model** one or all of the steps (shrug your own shoulders)
- Break down mult-step directions by doing **one step at a time** ("First, shrug your shoulder")

Teamwork

Don't go it alone! Bring in the team if your patient needs support outside your scope of practice.
- Neurology to manage symptoms related to brain injury
- Support groups or social groups (local or online)
- Gastrointestinal specialist for esophageal or digestive issues
- Otolaryngology for head, neck, ear, and throat concerns
- Occupational therapy for help with cognitive treatment, fine motor treatment, ADLs, IADLs, and adaptive equipment
- Physical therapy for positioning, functional mobility, and adaptive equipment
- Neuroopthamologist, ophthalmologist, or optometrist for vision and visuospatial concerns
- Audiologist and/or otolaryngologist for hearing concerns
- AAC company to set up device trials and help with troubleshooting
- Medical social work for community resources
- Mental health professionals to address mental health needs

Cueing Hierarchy for Naming Therapy

Naming therapy helps patients name words at the single-word level. Patients can use it to name pictured objects, objects in a room, or body parts. They may also work on naming verbs that are important to their lives (e.g., "eat," "stop," "brush").

This cueing hierarchy for expressive naming therapy progresses from minimal to maximal assistance. Prompt your patient to name the target. If they struggle, give a cue to help them succeed. Only move up the hierarchy (e.g. from description to sentence completion) if your patient continues to struggle to name the target word, even given previous cues. You may also add written cues (Caute et al., 2013; Sze et al., 2020; Marshall et al., 2012):

1. Give a **description** or **definition**.
   - For example, the target is the word "bed."
   - "This is something you sleep in."

2. Give a **sentence completion** cue.
   - "You sleep in a…"

3. Give a **semantically loaded sentence** completion cue.
   - "I put pillows and blanket on my…"

4. Give a **non-word rhyme**.
   - "It rhymes with the word 'ged.'"

5. Give an **initial sound** cue.
   - "It starts with 'buh,'" or "It starts with 'beh.'"

6. Give a **sentence completion cue** with the **rhyme** and **initial sound** cue.
   - "The name of this picture rhymes with 'ged' and starts with 'buh'. You sleep in a…'"

7. **Model** the word. Ask for repetition.
   - "The word is 'bed.' This is a…"

Environmental Modifications

Environmental modifications can improve a person with aphasia's safety, independence, and quality of life. Here are some helpful tips:

Improve the environment:
- Choose a quiet space with less background noise (Steffy et al., 2017).
- Choose supportive seating.
- Adjust the temperature and humidity for comfort.
- Make the space easier and safer to navigate: declutter, have clear walking paths, and label bins.

Make communication easier:
- Make sure everyone can see each other's faces: turn on more lights, get closer, and sit face-to-face.
- Encourage only one person to speak at a time.
- Save important conversations for when the person with aphasia has more energy.
- Use AAC, like an alphabet board, texting, or writing.
- Add visual supports, like labels, pictures, writing.
  - If you are printing, choose larger, sans-serif fonts, such as 14-point+ Arial font (Rose et al., 2011; 2003).
- Use video calls, like FaceTime or WhatsApp, instead of phone calls to add visuals.
- Encourage everyone to wear their hearing aids and glasses as needed.
- Use the free Telecommunication Relay Services, where an operator helps people with communication disorders make phone calls (National Relay Service in Australia, Relay U.K. in the United Kingdom).

Consider emergency communication:
- Have a quick way to call for help from a care partner inside the home, like a wireless doorbell or call chime.
- Have a quick way to call for help outside of the home, like text or personal emergency response system.
- Keep updated medical information on their phone or person.

Types of Aphasia

You often don't need to know the exact type of aphasia your patient has to provide effective treatment. If "expressive aphasia" is enough to make a functional treatment plan, go for it! However, you may choose to update the diagnosis to be more specific as you get to know your patient better. Here are the types of aphasia:

	Fluency	Comprehension	Repetition
Broca's	nonfluent	relatively intact	impaired
Wernicke's	fluent	impaired	impaired
Conduction	fluent	relatively intact	impaired
Transcortical Motor	nonfluent	relatively intact	relatively intact
Transcortical Sensory	fluent	impaired	relatively intact
Mixed Transcortical	nonfluent	impaired	relatively intact
Anomic	fluent	relatively intact	relatively intact
Global	nonfluent	impaired	impaired

Constraint-Induced Language Therapy

Constraint-induced language therapy (CILT) is an intensive treatment that encourages only verbal communication. It discourages ("constrains") all other modalities, including gesturing or writing. CILT aims to improve spoken language expression (Johnson et al., 2014; Taub, 2012). It was modeled after constraint-induced movement therapy, a well-regarded upper-limb rehabilitation treatment.

While CILT is proven to work, there are mixed findings about whether forcing verbal language adds value beyond the intensive practice (Raymer, 2023).

Because it's so intensive, this approach is not appropriate for all patients. To participate in CILT, a patient needs the motivation, stamina, and support to do intensive language training for 2-4 hours per day.

The 3 principles of constraint-induced language therapy
1. Forced use: Only speaking is allowed
2. Constraint: No compensations (no gestures, writing, or AAC)
3. Massed practice: Intensive practice for 2-4 hours per day, 5 days per week

Intensive practice ideas
1. Speech repetition drills (using words that are commonly difficult for people with non-fluent aphasia)
2. Activities-of-daily-living phrase repetition drills ("Is the coffee ready?")
3. Naming pictures game
4. Picture description
5. Role play of daily scenarios

Guidelines for CILT

Shape the patient's responses
- Make every task slightly more complex than your patient can do
- Make it progressively more difficult as they improve
- Give praise and encouragement
- Give breaks
- Only work on one variable at a time. For example, shape complexity (5-word sentence to 10-word sentence to multiple sentences) OR repetition (5+ photos to 10+ photos). But not both.

Keep up the intensity
- Time their responses and require progressively faster speech rates. Gamify by encouraging patients to beat their score
- Train care partners not to talk for your patient

Train care partners how to do CILT at home with the patient
- Encourage your patient and care partners to make a commitment that:
  - Your patient will speak as much as possible at home
  - The care partner will encourage verbal speech without helping too much
- Daily homework. Assign and ask your patient to track their home program

Verb Network Strengthening Treatment (VNeST)

VNeST improves word-finding and sentence production (Edmonds, n.d.) It may be a good starting point for your patients who have moderate expressive aphasia or chronic aphasia (Poirier, 2023) or for patients who seem to benefit from verbal or written input (Edmonds et al., 2009). VNeST was developed by Lisa Edmonds.

To do VNeST, the clinician presents a target verb. Your patient then builds sentences from this verb using "wh" questions. VNeST uses the terms "agent" for WHO and "patient" for WHAT.

Materials
- 10 familiar verbs. Each verb should:
  - Take an object ("arrive" won't work)
  - Be familiar but not too broad ("is" and "have" are too broad)
  - Be different from each other (don't choose both "throw" and "toss")
  - See below for more information
- Something to write with and write on:
  - Notecards/pen, portable whiteboard/marker, paper/pen, computer, or iPad
  - Whatever works best for each patient and yourself!
- Sentences for each verb (see below for more information)

Step 1. Write down WHO, WHAT, and the target verb, and place them in front of your patient.
- Ask them, "WHO can VERB?"
  - The answer should be specific to the verb. It can also be personal to your patient (for example, "My mom measures")
  - Clinician: "Who would measure something?"
  - Patient: "Carpenter"
- Ask, "WHAT can BE VERBED?"
  - The answer should be specific to the verb. For example, "Carpenter measures wood."
  - Clinician: "What's something the carpenter might measure?"
  - Patient: "Wood"

- Ask your patient to generate 3 scenarios for each target verb. The 3 scenarios shouldn't be too similar. For example:
  - Carpenter measures wood
  - My mom measures fabric
  - The chef measures ingredients

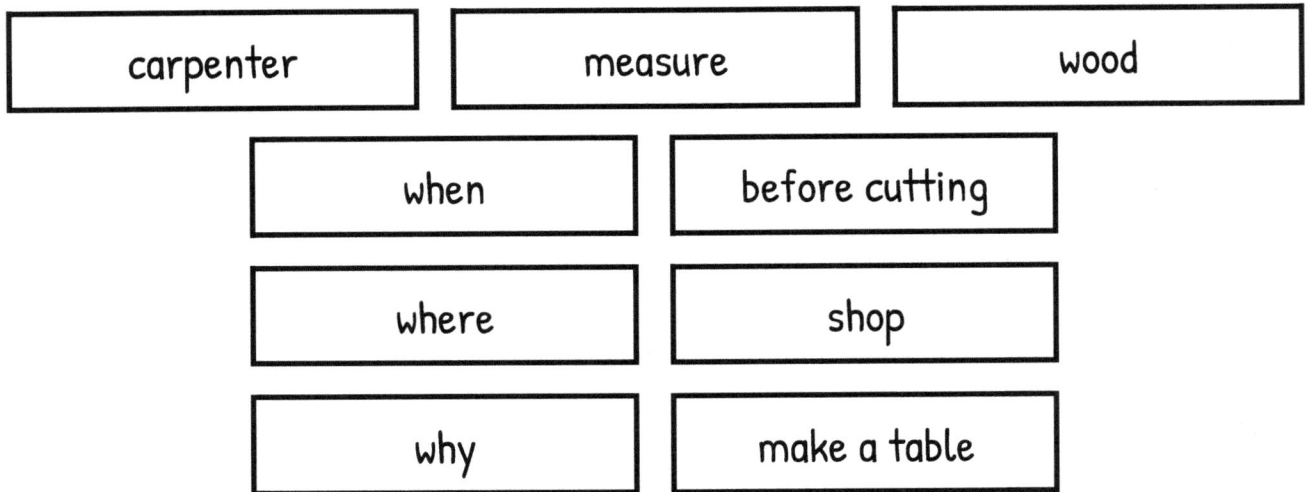

carpenter	measure	wood

when	before cutting
where	shop
why	make a table

Step 2. Your patient reads aloud the 3 sentences they just generated. They can read it independently, or you can provide support and cues as needed.

Step 3. Your patient chooses one of the 3 scenarios they came up with. For example, "My mom measures fabric"
- Write down WHERE, WHEN, and WHY. Ask WHERE, WHEN, and WHY questions about the scenario, and write down their answers.
  - Clinician: "WHERE does your mom measure fabric?"
  - Patient: "Table"
  - Clinician: "WHEN does your mom measure fabric?"
  - Patient: "At night"
  - Clinician: "WHY does your mom measure fabric?"
  - Patient: "Her job"
- Ask your patient to read aloud all of the sentences they just generated.
  - "My mom measures fabric at the table"
  - "My mom measures fabric at night"
  - "My mom measures fabric because it's her job"
  - Put them all together: "My mom measures fabric at the table at night because it's her job"

Step 4. Before the session, prepare 12 sentences containing the target verb. Read each sentence one at a time and ask your patient whether it makes sense.

- 3 sentences will be **correct.**
    - The carpenter measures wood. The chef measures ingredients. The designer measures fabric.
- 3 sentences will have the **wrong agent.**
    - The dentist measures wood. The policeman measures chemicals. The farmer measures clothes.
- 3 sentences will have the **wrong patient.**
    - The carpenter measures time. The scientist measures criminals. The designer measures teeth.
- 3 sentences will have the **agent and patient switched.**
    - The wood measures the carpenter. The chemical measures the scientist. The clothes measure the designer.

Step 5. Clear the table and ask what the target verb is. Next, ask them to name an agent(s) and a patient(s) again. Provide cues as needed, focusing on language and not memory.

- Therapist: "What verb were you just working on?"
- Patient: "Measure"
- Therapist: "Tell me again who might measure and what they would measure?"
- Patient: "My mom measures fabric"

VNeST ideas

Here are examples of 10 familiar verbs with WHO and WHAT words. For example, WHO saves something? An investor. WHAT do they save? Money.

SAVE
Investor/money
Lifeguard/swimmer
Shortcut/time

REPAIR
Mechanic/cars
Cobbler/shoes
Therapist/relationship

CARRY
Mother/infant
Criminal/guilt
Caddy/golf clubs

CUT
Chef/vegetables
Lumberjack/wood
Stylist/hair

DRILL
Coach/athletes
Dentist/teeth
Carpenter/board

FALL
Leaf/tree
Couple/love
Victim/prank

FRY
Pan/egg
Test/brain
Hairdryer/hair

LOSE
Players/game
Gambler/bet
Explorer/way

MIX
Artist/paint
Bartender/drink
Spoon/ingredients

OPERATE
Surgeon/heart
Owner/business
Technician/x-ray

Intention Manipulation

Intention manipulation is a treatment approach for moderate to severe expressive aphasia. It aims to improve expressive language by recruiting the right hemisphere of the brain.

Intention manipulation is not a stand-alone aphasia treatment. Rather, your patient performs a multi-step left-hand movement while doing a naming task. For example, they make circles with their left hand or use their left hand to open a box and press a button inside. Preliminary research suggests it may shift some language production to the right side of the brain (Crosson, 2008).

To do intention manipulation, your patient completes a left-hand movement during a naming task. Here's a general protocol:

1. Your patient completes a complex left-hand movement (e.g. they open the lid of a box and then squeeze a ball).

2. During the hand movement, ask them to name a target picture.

3. If correct, proceed to the next target picture.

4. If incorrect, your patient repeats the target word and then completes a different left-hand movement (e.g. making a circle with the left hand).

Melodic Intonation Therapy

Melodic Intonation Therapy (MIT) is a protocol that improves expressive language using repetition, tapping patterns, and intonation patterns (Norton et al., 2009; Zhang et al., 2022; Zumbansen et al., 2014).

MIT can successfully treat both nonfluent aphasia and acquired apraxia of speech (Sparks et al., 1974; Sparks & Holland, 1976; Zumbansen et al., 2014). This approach improves repetition and may improve functional communication and phrase length in people with non-fluent aphasia (Popescu et al., 2022; Zhang et al., 2022; Haro-Martínez et al., 2021).

MIT starts by increasing verbal output and functional communication. Essentially, you want your patient to be able to produce anything by speech. As they progress, you may switch the focus to increasing the length of utterances to phrases and sentences.

Candidates for melodic intonation therapy
The best candidates have most or all of the following (Norton, 2009):
- History of a unilateral, left-hemisphere stroke
- Nonfluent, severely restricted, or poorly articulated speech output
- Poor repetition at the single word level
- Ability to produce some intelligible words while singing familiar songs
- Moderately intact auditory comprehension
- Good motivation and good attention span

Example melodic intonation therapy protocol (Norton et al., 2009):

1. **Present the target phrase**
2. **Hum the phrase** at a rate of 1 syllable per second
   - Hum a higher-pitched note on the stressed syllable or word
   - For example, with the word "apple," the first syllable "ah" will be higher-pitched and the second syllable "ple" will be lower-pitched
3. **Sing the phrase twice while tapping.** While singing, you tap your patient's left hand on each syllable
   - Again, sing a higher-pitched note on the stressed syllable or word
4. **Sing the phrase in unison with your patient while tapping** their left hand on each syllable

5. **Continue to sing the phrase together while tapping** their left hand. Gradually fade your singing
   - Now, your patient is singing alone while you tap their left hand (don't give verbal or oral/facial cueing)
6. **Take turns singing while you keep tapping:** You sing the phrase while your patient listens
   - Stop singing so that your patient sings the phrase alone, but keep tapping their left hand
7. **Immediately after a correct production, ask, "What did you say?"** Tap your patient's hand as they sing the target phrase
8. **Repeat with a new phrase**

Functional phrase list that you can use with MIT:
1. Good morning!
2. Nice to meet you!
3. Thank you!
4. How are you?
5. I am tired.
6. I'm in pain.
7. I'm hungry.
8. I'm thirsty.
9. Bathroom please.
10. My name is _____.
11. See you later.
12. I love you!
13. What's new?
14. Let's go.
15. I don't know.

Response Elaboration Training

Response elaboration training (RET) aims to increase the number of words a person with aphasia says during a conversation. It doesn't have a protocol; rather, it encourages your patient to speak longer utterances by:
1. Confirming their responses, and then
2. Chaining onto (elaborating) their responses

RET can be beneficial for patients who (Bunker et al., 2019; Gaddie et al., 1991; Wambaugh et al., 2013):
- Have mild to moderate expressive aphasia
- May benefit from picture inputs or auditory prompts
- Are motivated to increase syntactic complexity

Here's an example of RET using a visual prompt:

1. Show the patient a picture
2. Say, "Tell me as much as you can about this picture"
   - For example, you show a picture of a man brushing his teeth
3. Your patient says, "Man...brushing"
4. Confirm your patient's response, then expand their utterance
   - "That's correct. The man is brushing his teeth"
5. Ask wh-questions to elicit more information
   - "What is he using to brush his teeth?"
6. Confirm what they say, then offer a longer sentence for them to imitate
   - "Yes! He's brushing his teeth with a toothbrush. What is he doing?"
7. Continue to elaborate with more wh-questions

Here's an example of RET using an auditory prompt:
An auditory prompt is another way to encourage more content words. It's also known as "modified" response elaboration training, or M-RET (Wambaugh, 2013).

For this prompt, you'll choose a multi-step functional task familiar to your patient, then ask them to describe how to do it. Examples are how to do a daily task, a hobby, a chore, etc.

1. Ask your patient the steps to doing a task
   - For example, "Describe in detail the steps to doing your laundry"
   - Your patient may respond with, "I sort clothes and put them in the washer"
2. Positively confirm what they say, then ask for more information
   - "That's right. Let's pretend that I've never done laundry before. Explain to me step-by-step what to do in detail"
3. Give your patient enough time to generate a longer response. After they stop speaking, ask, "Is there anything else?"
4. Repeat this process with additional auditory prompts

Other prompts for auditory stimuli:
Tell me in detail how you would...
- Buy groceries for dinner
- Take your medications
- Water your garden
- Buy a birthday present
- Feed a pet
- Visit your daughter
- Play Rummy (or another card game)

Semantic Feature Analysis

Semantic feature analysis (SFA) aims to improve word retrieval, especially of nouns. It uses a word chart that prompts patients to generate semantic information about a picture card. SFA is recommended for people who have at least some intact naming ability (Boyle, 2010; Efstratiadou et al., 2018; Maddy et al., 2014).

Semantic feature analysis works best for patients who:
- Have mild to moderate aphasia
- Have normal (or corrected) vision and hearing
- Don't have moderate to severe motor disorders
- Don't have comorbid cognitive impairments (i.e., memory, executive functioning impairment)

Materials
- Semantic feature analysis chart (on a whiteboard, paper, editable digital PDF, etc.)
- Images of target nouns

The chart includes 6 semantic features:
1. Association: What does the picture remind you of?
2. Group: What type of thing is it?
3. Action: What does it do?
4. Properties: What does it look/taste/sound/feel like?
5. Location: Where do you find it?
6. Use: What is it used for?

How to choose target nouns
- Interview your patient and/or their care partners to choose a list of words that are hard for them to say and meaningful to them.
- If that doesn't elicit enough words, add words to the list that you think are meaningful to your patient, such as daily activities, interests, etc.
- Try to gather nouns from a wide range of categories. For example, gather food, medical, gardening, and travel nouns.

Semantic feature analysis protocol:

1. Present the semantic feature analysis chart and a picture of the target noun.
2. Ask your patient to name the picture. Keep going, whether they name it correctly or not.
3. Prompt them to name the 6 semantic features on the chart, one by one. Write down their responses and cue as needed.
4. After they've named all 6 features, ask them to name the picture again.
5. Summarize the chart to prompt a correct answer.
   ○ For example, if the target picture is a boat, the summary may be, "It's a big vehicle that floats on water, looks like a canoe, and is used for fishing."
6. Use the same 10 pictures each session until your patient achieves 80% accuracy independently. Then, use 10 new pictures of nouns.

canoe	**vehicle**	**floats**
Association	Group	Action

Target word/picture

big	**water**	**fishing**
Properties	Location	Use

Semantic Feature Analysis Chart

Association	Group	Action

Target word/picture

Properties	Location	Use

Phonological Components Analysis

Like SFA, phonological components analysis (PCA) uses a word web to prompt patients to improve word retrieval. It is recommended for people who have some naming ability and may benefit from accessing phonological information (i.e., phonemes, word structure) about words (Leonard et al., 2008; Marcotte et al., 2018; van Hees et al., 2013).

Materials
- Phonological components analysis chart (on a whiteboard, paper, editable digital PDF, etc.)
- Images of target nouns

The chart includes 5 phonological components:
1. Rhyming word: What does the word rhyme with?
2. First sound: What's the first sound in the word?
3. Another word: What's another word that starts with that sound?
4. Final sound: What's the last sound in the word?
5. Number of syllables: How many syllables does the word have?

How to choose target nouns
- Interview your patient and/or their care partners to choose a list of nouns that are hard for them to say and are meaningful to them.
- If that doesn't elicit enough words, add words to the list that you think are meaningful to your patient, such as daily activities, interests, etc.
- Try to gather nouns from a wide range of categories. For example, gather food, medical, gardening, and travel nouns.

Phonological components analysis protocol:
1. Present the PCA chart and a picture of the target noun.
2. Ask your patient to name the picture.
3. One by one, ask them to name the 5 phonological components. Write down their responses.
   - If your patient can't generate a component, show and read a list of up to 3 choices for that component.
4. After they've named all 5 phonological components, ask them to name the picture again.

5. Summarize the chart to prompt a correct answer.
    ○ For example, if the target picture is a city, the summary may be, "It rhymes with the word 'kitty,' starts with the sound 's,' another word that starts with 's' is 'same,' it ends with 'e' and it has 2 syllables."
6. Use the same 10 pictures each session until your patient achieves 80% accuracy independently. Then, use 10 new pictures of nouns.

kitty	s	same
Rhymes with	First sound	Another word

Target word/picture

e	2
Final sound	Number of syllables

Example of phonological components analysis:
1. Target picture and word: City
2. "What is this a picture of?"
3. "What does the word rhyme with? Good try. Here's a clue. Does the word rhyme with cup, elevator, or kitty?" (Kitty)
4. "What's the first sound in the word?" (S)
5. "What's another word that starts with that sound?" (See)
6. "What's the last sound in the word?" (Y)
7. "How many syllables does the word have?" (2)
8. "So the word starts with the 's'-sound like the word 'see' and ends with the 'e'-sound. It rhymes with 'kitty' and has 2 syllables. What's the word?"

Phonological Components Analysis Chart

Rhymes with _____

First sound _____

Another word _____

Target word/picture _____

Final sound _____

Number of syllables _____

Supported Conversation for Adults with Aphasia

Supported Conversation for Adults with Aphasia (SCA™) is a treatment approach that aims to improve functional and social communication. It was developed by Aura Kagan and the Aphasia Institute. SCA improves communication by training the communication partner to acknowledge and reveal the person with aphasia's competence. You can use SCA with all severities of expressive or receptive aphasia and with patients who would benefit from multiple modalities (e.g. talking while using written cues and tapping keywords for emphasis; Kagan et al., 2001; Simmons-Mackie et al., 2016).

Train the communication partner to acknowledge competence:
- Treat the person with aphasia like an intelligent adult.
- Speak naturally and talk directly to the person.
- Use an adult tone of voice, words, and speech volume.
- Acknowledge and emphasize that you know that the person with aphasia knows more than they can currently communicate. For example, you can say, "I know that you know."
- Attribute communication breakdowns to your own limitations as a communicator.
- Be open if you have to turn to someone else to get information.

Train the communication partner to reveal competence:
- Make sure the topic of conversation is clear.
  - Use short, simple sentences.
  - Use a slow to normal speech rate.
  - Include visuals, like gestures, written keywords, and simple drawings.
  - Reduce distractions.
  - Observe your patient's non-verbal social cues (nodding, blank stare, etc.) to assess their level of comprehension.

- Make sure the person with aphasia can express themselves.
  - Ask yes/no questions.
  - Ask one question at a time.
  - Ask specific questions (versus open-ended).
  - Request more information by asking the person to gesture, point on an AAC board, write, etc.
  - Give them plenty of time to respond.

- Make sure that you understood each other.
  - Summarize what you believe the message is and ask for clarification. For example, you might say, "Let me make sure I understand," and then summarize what you heard.
  - Repeat the message.
  - Add gestures or write down keywords.
  - Expand what you think they were trying to say.
  - Summarize longer conversations.

(Aphasia Institute, n.d.)

Promoting Aphasic's Communicative Effectiveness

Promoting Aphasic's Communicative Effectiveness (PACE) uses multiple forms of communication and the back and forth of conversation to improve communication effectiveness. It's not a protocol but rather an approach to help patients get their message across. Use PACE with mild to moderate expressive aphasia.

First, your patient will choose which forms of communication to use (talking, writing, etc.), and then you and your patient take turns conveying messages in conversation.

PACE Rating Scale (Davis, 1980):
5   Message conveyed on first attempt
4   Message conveyed after general feedback from the clinician
3   Message conveyed after specific feedback from the clinician
2   Message partially conveyed **after** general and specific feedback
1   Message not conveyed despite general and specific feedback
0   Patient did not attempt to convey the message

How to do PACE:
- Traditionally, PACE is used with picture cards to expand on naming therapy. However, you can also use PACE in any practical conversation that your patient wants to have, such as saying their name and phone number or ordering at a restaurant.
- Your patient decides which forms of communication they'll use (speech, gestures, AAC, writing, etc.)
- Take equal turns during a conversation. For example, if you asked a question, now it's their turn to respond.
- After the conversation, give feedback about how clearly they conveyed their message.
- Teach the care partner how to take turns sending and receiving messages and how to give feedback about accuracy.

(Davis, 1980; Kurland et al, 2016)

Sentence Production Program for Aphasia

Sentence Production Program for Aphasia (SPPA) elicits target phrases using story completion via picture cards with action scenes. It can improve sentence-level expressive language. SPPA is recommended for patients with mild to moderate expressive aphasia who would benefit from picture inputs and are motivated to increase syntactic complexity.

To do SPPA, the clinician presents a picture card and reads a brief story that includes the target sentence structure. Next, the clinician asks a question that elicits the patient to repeat the target sentence. The patient then uses the same sentence structure to complete different narratives.

SPPA teaches patients to elicit 8 different types of sentences: imperative intransitive, imperative transitive, wh-interrogative, what & who, wh-interrogative, where & when, declarative transitive, declarative intransitive, comparative, and yes-no questions.

Nancy Helm-Estabrooks and Marjorie Nicholas created the SPPA program, and it is available for purchase online (Helm-Estabrooks & Nicholas, 2000).

SPAA example:
- Present the SPAA picture card and read the accompanying story.
  - "Andy is shopping at the mall. He tries on a blue shirt that he likes, but the price tag is missing. Andy asks an employee, 'How much does the shirt cost?'"
  - You ask the patient, "What does Andy ask the employee?"
  - Correct patient answer: "How much does the shirt cost?"
- For the next level of SPAA, you ask the patient, "When Andy doesn't know the shirt's price, what does Andy ask?"
  - Correct patient answer: "How much does the shirt cost?"
- Next, the patient uses this same sentence structure ("How much does the shirt cost?") to complete different narratives.

Treatment of Underlying Forms

Treatment of Underlying Forms (TUF) is a program that uses pictures and word cards to break down complex sentences into their parts. The goal of TUF is for patients to understand and then produce complex sentence structures, which will then generalize to the simpler sentences they use in everyday life (Swiderski et al., 2021). It is recommended for mild to moderate aphasia. The TUF program was developed by Cynthia Thompson and is sold online by Northwestern University (Thompson, 2001; Thompson & Shapiro, 2005).

TUF has different treatment protocols, depending on the type of sentence you want your patient to produce. We'll cover one of these protocols: The Object-extracted wh-questions (wh movement). You can learn TUF by purchasing the publisher's materials online.

Preparing for TUF:
1. Gather 10 pairs of picture cards. Each picture should have an ACTION with both a SUBJECT and an OBJECT. The pair of picture cards will have the same ACTION. But the OBJECT and SUBJECT will be reversed.
   - In the example pair below, the shared ACTION is "chases."
   - In Picture 1, the SUBJECT is the "dog," and the OBJECT is the "boy." The dog chases the boy.
   - In Picture 2, the **subject** is the "boy," and the OBJECT is the "dog." The boy is now chasing the dog.

Illustration copyright © 2023 Vince Aparo

Picture 1: the dog chases the boy   Picture 2: the boy chases the dog

2. Write down the SUBJECT and the OBJECT on separate notecards. Do this for each of the 10 pairs of pictures.

3. Write the verb describing the action in the picture pair on separate notecards. Do this for each of the 10 pairs of pictures.

4. On 8 separate notecards, write the following:
   - who
   - what
   - ?
   - it
   - was
   - by

Treatment of underlying forms protocol example:

1. Present the REVERSED pair.

Illustration copyright © 2023 Vince Aparo

2. Present the following notecards: SUBJECT, OBJECT, verb, who (and/or "what"), and ?
   - Place the boy (subject notecard), is, chasing (verb notecard), the dog (object notecard) in the correct order.

boy	is	chasing	dog

   - Place the who, ? (and/or "what") notecards above the sentence.

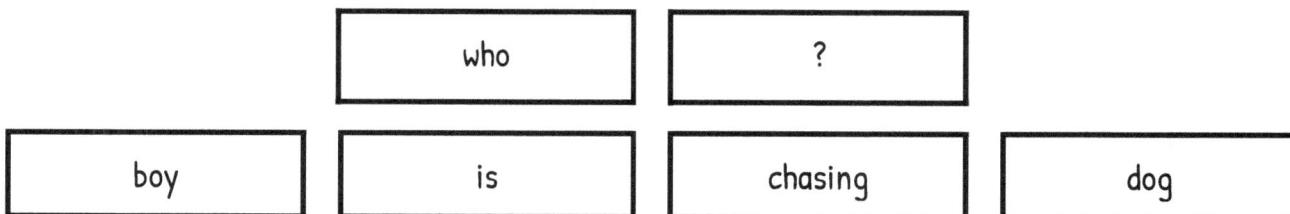

who	?

boy	is	chasing	dog

   - Point to the verb card and say, "This is chasing. It is the action of the sentence."
   - Point to the subject card and say, "This is the boy. He is the person doing the chasing."
   - Point to the object card and say, "This is the dog. It is being chased."

3. Replace the OBJECT with who (or "what").
    ○ Say, "The object is who (or 'what'), and they are being chased."
    ○ Place ? at the end of the sentence, then ask your patient to read (or repeat) the new sentence.
    ○ For example: boy, is, chasing, who, ?

boy	is	chasing	who	?

4. Move 'is' to the beginning of the sentence.

5. Then, move who (or "what") to the beginning of the sentence. Ask your patient to read (or repeat) the resulting question
    ○ who, is, boy, chasing, ?

who	is	boy	chasing	?

6. Rearrange the word cards to make a declarative sentence. The SUBJECT and OBJECT should now be switched
    ○ dog is chasing boy

dog	is	chasing	boy

7. Present the corresponding target picture.

Illustration copyright © 2023 Vince Aparo

8. Repeat steps 2-6.

9. Return to step 1 with a new target pair.

Treatment of Underlying Forms Cards

WHO	WHAT
?	IT
WAS	BY

Script Training

Script training aims to improve expressive language in daily conversations. Work with your patient to make scripts that will improve their daily life. For example, create a script to call the pharmacy for a medication refill or a script to order food. Each script should have at least 10 lines, with lines for both your patient and the conversation partner. Script training is recommended for patients with mild, moderate, and chronic expressive aphasia who want to say a monologue in specific situations (Kaye & Cherney, 2016; Hollo et al., 2024).

How to create scripts for your patients:

- Choose a script topic that's relevant to your patient
- Match the script level with your patient's aphasia severity
- As they improve, increase the readability difficulty (increase the number of syllables, words, then sentences in the script)
- As they improve, increase the syntactic difficulty (use complex vs. simple sentences)
- As they improve, increase the semantic difficulty (use more complex, less frequent, or longer words)
- Add in personalized content. For example, add in the name of their town or the name of a loved one

(Kaye & Cherney, 2016)

Kaye and Cherney's 2016 article, "*Script Templates: A Practical Approach to Script Training in Aphasia,*" provides examples of functional scripts with instructions for modifying them.

Aphasia Reading Treatments

Multiple Oral Re-Reading (MOR) & Modified Multiple Oral Re-Reading (MMOR)

MOR is an alexia treatment that aims to improve reading rate and accuracy. The modified version also targets reading comprehension. To do MOR, the patient re-reads the same text (a longer paragraph or short story) aloud multiple times until they meet a certain threshold of reading speed and accuracy. Once they reach that threshold, they move on to another passage. The clinician gives cues as needed. In the modified version, the clinician asks comprehension questions after the patient reads (Purdy et al., 2018). It's best to choose text with high-frequency words, because the words your patients practice reading most will improve the most (Lacey et al., 2010).

Oral Reading for Language in Aphasia (ORLA)

This reading treatment aims to improve reading fluency and whole-word recognition in patients who have severe aphasia (Purdy et al., 2018). ORLA uses a hierarchy of cues to help patients read sentences or paragraphs.

ORLA protocol hierarchy:
1. Read the sentence/paragraph aloud to your patient while pointing to each word.
2. Read and point as your patient points along.
3. Read in unison as you both point to the words. Repeat several times.
4. Say a word for your patient to identify in each sentence.
5. Point to a word in each sentence and ask your patient to name it.
6. Ask your patient to read the whole text in unison with you.

Supported Reading Comprehension

This approach aims to improve reading comprehension by adding supports.

Examples of supports to add to reading:
- Written keywords
- Photographs
- Aphasia-friendly formatting of text: lots of white space, large and standard fonts, simplified syntax and vocabulary (Dietz, 2014)

AAC

AAC

Your patient likely needs some form of AAC if they experience any of the following:
- Unable to fully express their wants, needs, thoughts, and feelings by talking
- They have severe dysarthria or apraxia of speech or are intubated
- Their speech rate drops below 125 WPM
- They are fatigued or frustrated when communicating by talking

Buy-In
Make sure that your patient is willing and able to learn to communicate by means other than talking. They may also need a dedicated facilitator (main communication partner or care partner) who is willing and able to support their use of AAC.

To improve buy-in, educate them on what AAC is, how it might help them, and what it may look like for them.

The AAC Process
AAC treatment starts by adding vocabulary and learning the new pace and rhythm of conversation. If relevant, you'll also teach the technical skills of using a high-tech device. Start with short, structured exchanges and build from there.

First, help your patient communicate their immediate wants and needs. As you teach them how to select a message, you can also show them how to navigate the device and add vocabulary.

Next, focus on communicating their thoughts and feelings. Help them build a library of messages with their favorite topics of conversation. These may include hobbies, interests, favorite sports teams, etc. Teach strategies that will help them during social exchanges, like how to signal that they want to communicate and what to do if communication breaks down.

Throughout treatment, encourage your patient to use any communication modality that works! They aren't limited to one system, even a high-tech device, if a simpler modality is just as effective. For example, they can look left for "no" and right for "yes" instead of selecting symbols on a screen.

For people used to natural speech as their primary means of communication, AAC will likely feel limiting—it's much slower, and a device can only hold so many pre-made messages. Part of your patient and facilitator education will be acknowledging the differences (and cons!) of using AAC.

That said, you, your patient, and the facilitator can build a system of messages that covers your patient's communication needs. From small talk to emergency information to discussing philosophy (or reality TV).

Teamwork.

Don't go it alone! Bring in the team if your patient needs support outside your scope of practice.

- Occupational therapy for fine motor control, ADLs, IADLs, adaptive equipment, and positioning
- Physical therapy for positioning, functional mobility, and adaptive equipment
- Neurology for help managing any underlying neurological impairmen
- AAC company for device trials and tech support
- Diagnosis-specific referrals (e.g., registered dieticians to manage hydration and nutrition, neuro-ophthalmologist to manage visual neglect or field cuts)

Environmental Modifications

Environment modifications can make it easier for someone using AAC to communicate.

Improve the space
- Choose a quiet space with good acoustics and minimal background noise
- Have good lighting that's not too bright or too dim
- Avoid glare on the AAC screen

Make communication easier
- Sit upright and choose supportive seating
- Have a portable AAC option, like a card with high-frequency messages on one side and an alphabet board on the other
- Make sure everyone can see each other's faces: turn on more lights, get closer, and sit face-to-face
- Encourage only one person to speak at a time
- Save important conversations for when the patient has more energy
- Use video calls, like FaceTime or WhatsApp, instead of phone calls for the added visuals
- Encourage everyone to wear their hearing aids and glasses as needed

Have an emergency communication plan (Brownlee, 2021; Costello & O'Brien, n.d.)
- Keep non-tech rapid access AAC nearby, like an alphabet board or eye-gaze board with a laser pointer
- Have a quick way to call for help from a care partner inside the home, like a wireless doorbell or call chime
- Have a quick way to call for help outside of the home, like email, text, social media, or a personal emergency response system
- Have updated medical information on their phone
- Encourage using wearable medical information like a medical wristband or lanyard

Augmented Input

Augmented input is an AAC strategy that increases language comprehension by adding visual information.

"Augmented" means extra, and "input" is visual information. This means that you'll add visual information as you speak. For example, as you speak, you'll also write, draw, point, gesture, or use pictures. The goal is for your patient to better understand what you're saying.

Augmented input is especially helpful when your patient is learning how to use a new AAC device. Add visual input to help them understand what a symbol means, especially if they have a more severe cognitive impairment.

For example, a patient doesn't understand that the picture of a plate with food on it means "meal." To use augmented input, you point to the "meal" symbol and ask, "What do you want to eat?" while acting out eating something.

Augmented Input Ideas
- Write out the message or keyword
- Draw the message
- Point to what the symbol represents (for example, point to the toilet symbol, then point to the restroom)
- Act out what the symbol represents (for example, point to the toothbrush symbol, then act out brushing your teeth)
- Show photos or pictures that the message is connected to (for example, point to the bathtub symbol, then show a photo of soap and shampoo)

Core Vocabulary Approach

"Core vocabulary" makes up around 80% of what people say everyday, and are mostly verbs, adjectives, pronouns, and prepositions. Core vocabulary isn't context-specific, which mean that the words can be used in many different situations (e.g., "be," "no"). There is also "fringe vocabulary," which are primarily context-specific nouns, such as "dinner" and "plate" (Witkowski & Baker, 2012).

The core vocabulary approach starts by first teaching a patient these core, high-frequency words as the foundation of their AAC language skills. Having core vocabulary allows them to ask and answer questions, describe, make requests, etc. You can then add on fringe vocabulary.

Many AAC devices' built-in vocabularies are based on core vocabulary. The core vocabulary should stay in the same location on an AAC board or device to make it easier for the patient to remember and motor plan. For example, a set of core words will stay on the same screen or in the same place on a page.

Here are some of the highest-frequency English words for adults that may be part of your patient's core vocabulary (from Shin et al., 2021):

- Be
- I
- You
- It
- The
- Not
- Do
- Have
- And
- A
- That
- To
- They
- There

- Yeah
- He
- Get
- She
- Oh
- What
- Well
- We
- Go
- In
- Say
- Know
- Of

- No
- Will
- But
- For
- Think
- Yes
- Can
- On
- So
- Mm
- Just
- This
- Then

Using Scales for Communication

A simple visual, such as a scale, can help a person using AAC to communicate more effectively during conversations (Beukelman, 2012).

You can use scales in many conversations, such as:
- How they slept last night
- What their opinion was about a movie
- What their pain level is
- How much they want to do something, and more!

How To Use A Scale For Communication
1. Start a conversation and ask an open-ended question.
   - For example, you talk about your morning and then ask, "How did you sleep last night?"
2. Draw a scale and write 2 or more words on the scale.
   - For example, "Terrible; Fine; Great."
3. Ask them to point to their answer.
4. Confirm their answer.
5. Ask more follow-up questions.
   - For example, they pointed to "Terrible," so you ask, "How many hours did you sleep?" and draw a new scale as needed.

Example scales:

How did you sleep last night?

Terrible ← Fine → Great

How's your pain?

No pain at all (0 1 2 3 4 5 6 7 8 9 10) Worst Pain

How enthusiastic do you feel about going on a walk today?

Not at all ← Neutral → Completely

Written Choice

Written choice is a strategy for patients with language comprehension deficits. It helps them better understand conversations and make choices.

General steps of written choice:
1. Start the conversation, then ask an open-ended question. "What would you like to do this weekend?"
2. Write down 2-4 choices. You can include an "other" option. For example, "Park. Store. Friend's house. Other."
3. Ask them to make their choice.
4. Confirm their choice.

You can then ask follow-up questions. For example, "You want to go to a store. What store do you want to visit?" Then, write down 2-4 more choices.

Example of written choice:

<u>What to do this weekend?</u>

Park   (Store)   Friend's house   Other

<u>Which store?</u>

Corner grocer   Farmer's Market   Other

Energy Conservation for AAC

Using AAC while living with a neurodegenerative disease or recovering from an injury can be exhausting. Introduce energy conservation strategies when communicating whenever your patient needs it (Tomik, 2010; Fateh et al., 2022):

Energy conservation strategies during communication include:
- Being in a quiet environment with distractions removed
- Improving breath support by sitting as upright as possible
- Positioning people face-to-face to allow for reading lips, facial expressions, gestures, etc.
- Taking rest breaks.
- Saving important conversations for when they have more energy or a better environment
- Using a portable, hands-free amplifier
- Sitting instead of standing
- Encouraging a healthy sleep schedule and diet to maximize energy

AAC Systems

There are many options for AAC systems, from pointing to texting to speech-generating devices. If the AAC system you choose helps your patient communicate their wants and needs and they're willing and able to try it, you're usually good to go.

However, there are extra considerations for some degenerative diseases or other significant impairments. For example, if you recommend a speech-generating device for a patient with ALS, ensure that it has an eye-gaze selection option.

Here are questions that can help you choose an appropriate AAC system for your patient. We'll review each in detail below.
- What type of AAC will they use now? And later?
- How will they formulate their messages now? And later?
- What foundational abilities do they have now? And later?
- How do they select a message now? And later?
- What kind of physical support do they need now? And later?
- What messages should be included?
- Why and how often do they need AAC now? And later?
- How can they communicate faster now?
- How will messages be displayed?

What Type of AAC Will They Use Now? And Later?

It's important to consider the type of AAC your patient needs now compared to in the future. Is AAC only for short-term use, like while recovering from a surgery? Will they need higher levels of AAC in the future due to a degenerative disease? Will they need alternative access, like eye gaze technology? Choose a system robust enough to meet their communication needs while balancing cost and complexity.

- **Unaided AAC:** They use their body to communicate (gesturing)
- **Aided AAC:** They use something external to communicate (a notepad, speech-generating device)
- **No technology AAC:** Unaided (gestures, facial expressions, pointing, finger spelling)
- **Low technology AAC:** Aided (pen and paper, whiteboard)
- **High technology AAC:** Aided (laptop, tablet, speech generating device)

The Adult Speech Therapy Protocols Pack

How Will They Formulate Their Messages Now? And Later?

Consider your patient's current physical and cognitive ability to formulate a message. Will this change in the future? This is especially important for patients with degenerative diseases like ALS. Now and in the future, can they:

- Type an entire message out
- Press one button for each word
- Press one button per phrase or pre-written monologue
- Select with a switch or head mouse
- Select with eye-gaze

What Foundational Abilities Do They Have Now? And Later?

Consider your patient's foundational abilities. How is their:

- **Language:** talking, listening, writing, reading
- **Technical skills:** ability to use technology
- **Cognition:** executive functioning, memory, and attention abilities needed to navigate, use, and troubleshoot the system
- **Social skills:** taking turns, using and understanding gestures, asking for clarification, and managing communication breakdowns

How Do They Select A Message Now? And Later?

How your patient selects a message will depend in part on their physical abilities (e.g. ability to control their hands), preferences, and the capabilities of their AAC system.

- **Direct:** Selecting a message directly via touch, eye gaze, head mouse, laser, etc.
- **Indirect:** Selecting a message by scanning for it among a set of choices. They may scan in a circular motion, line by line, row and column, item in category, etc. This may be needed by patients with severe physical limitations.

What Kind Of Physical Support Do They Need Now? And Later?

OT, PT, and other team members can help your patient get proper physical support for their hips, legs, arms, torso, and neck. Your patient should be supported but have the freedom to adjust their movements in order to communicate.

What Messages Should Be Included?

You'll continually add, subtract, and edit the messages on your patient's AAC system. Messages may include (Costello, 2016):

- The most useful premade/factory-set messages on the AAC device

The Adult Speech Therapy Protocols Pack   81

- Messages about emotions/feelings/moods ("I feel sad," "I'm frustrated," "This is incredible!")
- Requests for help/assistance ("Can you get that?" "May I get help?")
- Conversation repair messages ("What was that last part?" "I don't understand. Can you say that again?")
- What family and friends report they usually say
- What your patient isn't able to say yet (keep a running list in a communication journal)
- What your patient needs in a typical day
- What your patient would need to say in case of an emergency

Why And How Often Do They Need AAC Now? And Later?

For now (and, if applicable, in the future), consider the following:
- **Frequency.** How frequently will they need AAC?
  - Only during communication breakdowns
  - When tired at the end of the day
  - When speaking with unfamiliar listeners
  - Only in certain environments
  - All the time
- **Amount**
  - To supplement speech
  - As the primary means of communication
- **Purpose**
  - Communicate basic wants and needs
  - Socialize
  - Longer discussions (gossip, stories, collaboration with providers)

How Can They Communicate Faster Now?

Using AAC is roughly 20 times slower than speech (Beukelman et al., 2007). Increasing speed can benefit both your patient and their communication partners. Ways to communicate faster:
- Gestures
- Codes (i.e. TY for thank you)
- Acronyms
- Autocorrect
- Text predictions
- Text replacement
- Store messages in notepads or devices
- Premade scripts and monologues
- Premade templates

How Will Messages Be Displayed?

The display isn't likely to change significantly once you find a system that's a good fit for your patient. Any display should be easy for your patient to navigate. What to consider when choosing a display:

- Size of messages: button size, text size, etc.
- Number of messages per display page
- Organization of messages: location on the display, spacing between messages

Messages on AAC Device

AAC messages require constant updating. Some messages will be edited, some deleted, and some added. Let your patient and their facilitator know that this process is normal. After all, none of us can predict with 100% certainty what we'll say on a given day.

A practical way to update messages is to communicate with the device and then make changes after the exchange.

How To Decide What Messages To Include

Know your patient's daily schedule, from the moment they wake up to the moment they go to bed. Consider what messages they might need for each activity.

Take an inventory of the people they talk to in their different roles. In their personal lives, this may be family, friends, service and healthcare providers, and even people they pass on the street. In their professional lives, it may include coworkers, customers, and bosses. Think of what messages they may need for each role.

Also take inventory of where they go (physician's office, cafe, grocery store, community center, church, etc). Work with the patient and facilitator and use your best judgment to develop messages they may need to say in each setting.

Monologues

Add monologues to AAC systems to help patients communicate about themselves. Create messages for information they often repeat and topics that come up occasionally but are difficult to gesture or spell out quickly. You can also add monologues for things that are fun or meaningful for the person to communicate.

Here are some example monologues:

Introductions
"I had a stroke, and now I have aphasia, which is a language disorder. I can understand you, but I have a hard time coming up with words. I communicate using..."

Career
"I was a Park Ranger at North Cascades National Park. In the summer, I worked at the Visitor's Center. In the winter, I maintained the trails by chopping fallen trees into smaller pieces and moved them off trail."

Family
"I have three daughters and one son. The son is the youngest. They all live in California. My two eldest daughters are occupational therapists. The other daughter is a speech therapist. My son is a physical therapist. But I am not a therapist!"

Location
"I grew up in Houston, Texas. Some of my neighbors worked for NASA, and one of them was an astronaut on the Apollo missions. Houston summers are very hot and humid. We sometimes got hurricanes and tropical storms. My favorite part of Houston is The Heights because of the beautiful old houses and oak trees."

High-Tech Device Trials

If your patient needs a speech-generating device or other high-tech AAC, they'll likely trial a few options before finding the right fit.

Researching and trialing high-tech AAC options can be time-consuming. Talk to your employer about being compensated for the time you'll spend on this necessary task.

Purpose Of Device Trials

Speech-generating devices are often expensive and may only be covered by insurance every few years. Do trials to find the best fit for your patient. The device they choose should help them meet their communication goals while being something they and their facilitator are willing to use. Sometimes, the only way you'll know if a device checks these boxes is to try it!

Device Options

Here are some high-tech AAC options. However, since technology changes quickly, do your research. Options include:

- Your patient's own tablet or cellphone
- PRC-Saltillo
- Tobii DynaVox
- Lingraphica®
- Megabee Assisted Communication and Writing Tablet
- Enabling Devices
- FAB (Frenchay Alphabet Board) Keyboard
- GoTalk
- AbleNet, Inc.

Apps Options

Some options include:
- Verbally (free) or Verbally premium
- Co-Writer
- CoughDrop
- Speech Assistant
- Vocable AAC
- Weave Chat AAC
- Proloquo
- PredictAble
- LetMeTalk
- Flipwriter

Alternative Access Options

Alternative access allows your patient to use a device when they can no longer use their hands or body like they could before (Brownlee, 2021). There are alternative access options for speech-generating devices and Apple and Android products.

- **Eye-gaze:** A tool that uses eye-gaze to control a device
  - For speech-generating devices: Tobii Dynavox, PRC-Saltillo, Eyegaze Inc., Forbes AAC, EyeTech Digital
  - Apps for Apple products: Skyle, I Have a Voice, Hawkeye, Predictable AAC, Jabberwocky
  - For computers: Camera Mouse, Tobii PC Eye, Eye On by Eye Tech Digital, Eye Control on Microsoft Windows
- **Switches:** A piece of equipment (lever, button, mouth tube, etc.) that controls a device:
  - Tecla Shield for iPad
  - RJ Cooper (iPad adapter for switch)
- **Mouth sticks or head sticks:** Joysticks controlled by using the mouth or head movements
  - RJ Cooper
- **Headmouse:** replaces a standard computer mouse to control a device

Device Trial Providers

AAC manufacturers like Tobii offer device trials. Your patient's insurance usually covers the trials.

There are a growing number of lending libraries that offer free trials of AAC devices and alternative access. Check online for local device lending libraries.

Trials Cost

Device trials are often complimentary, but always check with your patient's insurance company and the device company before requesting a trial.

High-Tech Device Cost

High-tech devices can cost between several hundred to several thousand dollars. Speech-generating devices are considered durable medical equipment and are covered by Medicare, Medicaid, and some private insurance companies for eligible patients.

Check for local charities and nonprofits that offer free or low-cost speech-generating devices.

Ordering A Device To Trial

First, narrow down 2-4 devices to trial. When choosing a device, consider the following:
- Your patient's communication needs and weaknesses: how much support they need, how frequently, for how long
- Their communication strengths
- Their motor abilities: eye gaze, hand, finger, arm, neck and trunk strength and control
- Their sensory abilities: vision and hearing
- Cognitive abilities
- Technical skills
- Motivation and willingness to learn a new device
- Cost and funding source

To review the device with your patient and their facilitator, print out information or look at websites and videos together.

Once they've chosen a device to trial, contact their funding source, the device manufacturer, and/or an AAC lending library to borrow the device.

Device Trials

Once your patient has the loaned speech-generating device, ask them to:
- Locate specific symbols and folders
- Match symbols to words
- Type words, phrases, and sentences
- Have basic conversations
- Role-play everyday scenarios

Signs That A Device Is A Good Match

- Your patient uses it to communicate effectively
- They can navigate it with minimal or no frustration
- They can afford the device (or can secure funding)
- They make progress in speed and/or complexity of messages during the trial period

If the device is a good match and the patient wants to buy it/keep it, then communicate with device manufacturers, funding sources, or charities about the next steps.

If it's not a good match, identify why before sending the device back. You may be able to problem solve the issue before giving up on the device.

AAC for Aphasia

AAC can support communication in people with receptive or expressive aphasia (Burton et al., 2023). Here is a 4-step process for using AAC to improve communication in people with aphasia.

1. Introduce AAC

Severe or profound aphasia
Focus on communicating basic wants and needs.
- At this level, focus AAC treatment on gesturing and pointing to physical things in the environment rather than on images. For example, teach them to point to the restroom if they need the toilet or to act out eating if hungry. Connecting images to real-life objects may be too difficult for people with severe aphasia.
- Add context to improve comprehension. For example, talk only about meal-related items and actions during a meal.

Moderate aphasia
Use gestures to communicate about functional tasks, such as activities of daily living and meeting basic wants and needs.
- Encourage making choices (what to eat, what to wear, what music to listen to).
- Practice turn-taking (ask simple yes/no questions to encourage participation).
- Teach communication agreement or rejection (pointing, nodding, shaking head, etc.)

2. Increase Socialization

Once your patient with aphasia can use AAC to communicate basic wants, needs, and ADLs, work on increasing language comprehension and social engagement. AAC treatment will focus on adding visual supports and expanding gestures.

- Use augmented input. Do this by adding a lot of context, like drawing, writing, or pointing to symbols on an AAC board while talking.
- Expand gestures to communicate preferences, to more complex turn-taking, and to conversations. Ask simple, open-ended questions to encourage participation.

- Save time and energy by keeping a notepad or notes app to refer to previous conversations and choices, especially for frequently asked questions. For example, "What do you want for dinner?" or "How's your pain?"

3. Expand Communication Range

Once comprehension and social engagement increase, focus AAC treatment on expanding the range and depth of communication. Focus on hobbies, interests, jobs, friends, and other things that are important to them.

- Add a speech-generating device if needed. Your patient now has the attention and symbol recognition to use it.
    - Add monologues about aphasia. For example, "I have aphasia, which is a language disorder. I understand what you're saying, but speaking is difficult for me."
    - Add monologues about AAC. For example, "This device helps me communicate. Please be patient and give me extra time."
    - Add monologues about other useful conversation topics, like interests, the weather, etc.
- Have conversations and role-play to improve communication accuracy and speed.
- Encourage initiating conversations and sharing their experiences with generated speech or photos.

4. Increase Independence

Now that your patient has an expanded range of communication, you can focus aphasia AAC treatment on further increasing independence.

- Continue to build up their library of messages. Add topics that come up occasionally but are difficult to gesture or spell out quickly.
- Continue to role-play. Or leave the treatment room for real-world interactions!
- Identify communication breakdowns and teach strategies for repair.
- Make scripts for frequent interactions with multiple steps, such as scheduling a van pickup.

AAC for Inpatient Settings

All patients need a way to communicate their basic wants and needs. Patients who experience a sudden loss of speech (like after intubation, surgery, or trauma to the chest, neck, or head) need AAC that's quick and easy to learn.

Types of AAC
Inpatients often only need temporary AAC, so use what's readily available.
- Gestures, like pointing, thumbs up/down, nodding/shaking head.
- Writing or drawing.
- Simple AAC boards, like a needs board or alphabet board.
- Phone, tablet, or laptop for texting, word document, notes app, or AAC app.

Care team education
- Always use AAC when talking to the patient, even for yes/no questions.
- Keep boards in a plastic sleeve for easy sanitization.
- Keep the AAC board/device stored in the same place and within the patient's reach.
- Teach communication partner tips (they should give plenty of time, ask one question at a time, etc.)
- Use visual and written materials whenever possible. For example, bring a menu and ask your patient to point to their breakfast choice.

Patient education
Teach communication techniques. For example:
- How to get someone's attention.
- How to request no interruptions while they communicate.
- How to signal that someone misunderstood their message
- How to repair communication breakdowns.

AAC for ALS

Almost everyone who has ALS will develop dysarthria (most often mixed flaccid-spastic; Tomik & Guiloff, 2010). By the end of their lives, most won't be able to communicate by speaking, so AAC will be crucial for them. Start the discussion about AAC early, even on assessment day.

Hit the ground running

You'll likely (hopefully!) start seeing your patient with ALS while they still have natural speech. At the beginning of treatment, discuss the following:
- The progression of the disease, including loss of speech and other motor abilities.
- AAC and alternative access they may need in the future.
- When to trial speech-generating devices—typically once they have speech changes or even earlier.
- Message banking and voice banking.

Monitor speech rate and intelligibility

To increase comprehensibility, introduce:
- A personal amplifier.
- Clear speech strategies like over-articulation.
- Alphabet board and other AAC.

If you haven't already, trial speech-generating devices once their speech rate decreases to 125 words per minute or lower.

Know their participation and communication needs

Write down your patient's daily schedule, personal and professional roles, and daily interactions to create useful messages.
- You'll update these messages as your patient's roles and routines change throughout the course of their disease.
- Have an emergency communication plan in place for how to call for help and communicate if their high-tech device isn't working.

Consider cognitive, motor, and sensory changes
- Many people with ALS will have cognitive decline, including dementia or frontal lobe dysfunction. Keep this in mind as you choose strategies and modify their AAC systems.
- Patients with spinal onset may need alternative access methods earlier than those with bulbar onset.

- Most people (over 60%) with ALS have spinal onset. This means that the ALS symptoms first appear in their arms or legs. Symptoms include muscle cramps, weakness, and twitching.
- Bulbar-onset ALS first shows symptoms in the face or neck and tends to progress faster than spinal onset (Segura et al., 2023; Greenwood, 2020).

Late-stage support

- As your patient reaches the end stages of their disease, continue to modify their AAC systems, alternative access, and communication strategies as needed.
- Focus on helping your patients and their facilitators communicate their top wants and needs as easily as possible (Costello & O'Brien, n.d.)

Message & Voice Banking for ALS

Message Banking™

Message banking is the process of recording a patient's voice to capture their important messages while also preserving the sound of their voice. Patients ultimately create a library of personalized messages that they can play, even after losing their voice.

Preserving a patient's voice before they lose vocal speech can help them maintain a sense of self and better connect with others. These messages may be practical and/or meaningful words, phrases, sentences, sounds, and stories. Boston's Children's Hospital, in collaboration with Tobii Dynavox, offers free message banking for patients at mymessagebanking.com.

Voice Banking

With voice banking, your patient records samples of their natural speaking voice. These samples are used to create a custom, synthesized voice that can later be uploaded into a speech-generating device. Visit the ALS Association at als.org for more information about voice banking.

Message and voice banking take time and energy, so recommend them early, while patients' voices are more intelligible and they have the energy to record.

Fluency

Fluency

How you approach fluency treatment will depend on the type of fluency disorder, whether it was acquired or childhood-onset, and personal factors such as goals and levels of anxiety around stuttering. Treatment options for acquired fluency disorders are generally the same as those for childhood-onset fluency disorders. If childhood-onset, it's important to consider the patient's lifelong experience with stuttering and any secondary behaviors and negative reactions. Take the time to build a strong rapport. For all adult patients, managing any anxiety around stuttering is key to treatment success (Plexico et al., 2005).

Treat an acquired stutter if it persists for more than a week (Duffy, 2013), it impacts communication, and your patient is motivated to try treatment. Speech modification strategies are usually the best option (Brignell et al., 2020). However neurogenic stuttering generally doesn't respond well to fluency-inducing techniques, such as prolonged speech or choral reading.

Another factor to consider is pharmaceuticals. Some drugs can cause neurogenic stuttering, while others can treat it. If you notice a change in your patient's fluency that began within a few weeks of starting a new medication or shortly after stopping a drug, refer to their physician, pharmacist, and/or neurologist.

Teamwork

Don't go it alone! Bring in the team if your patient needs support outside your scope of practice.

- Pharmacist for medication management (medications that reduce stutter-like speech or cause medication-induced stuttering)
- Mental health professional to address mental health needs
- Neurologist to manage any underlying neurological impairment
- Stuttering or diagnosis-specific support groups (stroke, TBI) for social support

Camperdown Program

The Camperdown Program is a stuttering treatment for adults and older teens with mild to severe stuttering. It uses slow and exaggerated speech to increase fluency and has good evidence that it improves stuttering (Brignell et al., 2020; Laiho et al., 2022). The University of Technology Sydney offers training programs and free guides online. Here's a general outline (O'Brian et al., 2024):

1. **Introduce the program.** Your patient will learn a fluency technique to control (but not cure) their stutter. They must also practice with a dedicated communication partner outside of treatment.

2. **Teach the fluency technique.** Model or play an audio recording of this slow, exaggerated speech (available on the Camperdown Program website).

3. Ask your patient to **read in unison with the recording** while imitating the sample as closely as possible. The samples are usually passages, so start sentence-by-sentence or even phrase-by-phrase.

4. Record your patient **reading the passage aloud independently.** They listen to themselves and then answer self-reflection questions.

5. To increase generalization, your patient practices the **fluency technique with a hierarchy of tasks**, from easiest to hardest (read aloud, describe pictures, say a monologue, and then have a conversation).

6. Once your patient is proficient in using this technique of slow, exaggerated speech, teach them the **Fluency Technique Scale**. This scale quantifies how much technique they use during speech, ranging from no technique to very slow, exaggerated speech.

7. The following stages aim to develop **more natural-sounding speech** while maintaining fluency. To achieve this balance, patients move down the Fluency Technique Scale.
   - They listen to a recording of the next level on the Fluency Technique Scale.
   - Then, they practice this level with a hierarchy of tasks (reading aloud, describing a photo, saying a monologue, question-and-answer, conversation). Each time, they listen to a recording of themselves and answer self-reflection questions.
   - Once they reach a certain level of accuracy, they move down the Fluency Technique Scale to more natural-sounding speech that uses less technique.

8. In the following stages, they work towards **controlling their stutter in everyday speaking**.
   - They practice more complex conversations that fit their interests and needs, like ordering their morning tea or introducing themselves at a work holiday party.
   - They continue to record, listen, and self-reflect.

9. The final stage is **maintenance**, with the goal of maintaining the balance between controlling their stutter and speaking naturally in the long term.

Rate Control

Rate control strategies slow down the overall rate of speech. A slow speech rate, like pacing using a metronome, can improve speech coordination and fluency (Ingham et al., 2012).

Start by asking your patient to read one syllable at a time at a slow rate. The goal is to gradually work toward a natural-sounding speech rate during conversation.

Rate Control Strategies

- Speak at a slower rate.
- Insert more pauses while speaking, such as after each word or at the end of a phrase.
- Use a metronome and pace yourself to the beat.
- Use a pacing board and pace yourself to the movement of your finger.

Choral Speech and Shadowing

Choral speech involves reading aloud with your patient. Shadowing involves reading aloud as your patient repeats what you read, starting a few seconds after you.

Start by reading a sentence or paragraph aloud in unison. Encourage your patient to use their fluency strategies. The goal is for you to gradually fade reading so that your patient is reading alone. You can also record yourself reading and ask your patient to match the speech rate and breath groups.

Negative Reactions Management

Adult patients with chronic fluency disorders may have strong negative reactions to their stutter. They may experience decreased self-confidence, activity limitations, or even social phobias. The following treatments address the negative reactions that come with stuttering.

Increase Awareness

Increasing awareness of their overall speech and communication can help patients better understand their thoughts, feelings, and physical reactions around stuttering. It can also help them identify their specific speech strengths and weaknesses. Patients can increase awareness using strategies similar to stuttering modification (Van Riper, 1973):

- Identify other aspects of their speech and communication besides stuttering, including:
  - When they're fluent or use "easy" stuttering
  - When they use strategies
- Name thoughts, feelings, and behaviors (blinking, clenching fist, etc.) before, during, and after each disfluency.
- Name thoughts, feelings, and behaviors about their speech and their identity as a communicator.

General tips for promoting self-awareness:

- Right before the stutter: What happens in their body and where? What do they think and feel?
- During the stutter: What happens in their body and where? What do they think and feel?
- After the stutter: What happens in their body and where? What do they think and feel?
- Fluent speech: What happens in their body and where? What do they think and feel?
- Make a plan for what to do before, during, and after stuttering. Help your patient identify what strategies work best for them (e.g., box breathing, easy onset, self-disclosure).

Promote Mindfulness

Mindfulness is being aware of the present moment, including thoughts and feelings. It's an evidence-based way to improve speech fluency and mental health (Beilby, 2012).

Mindfulness can decrease negative reactions in people who stutter. By pausing to identify how they feel, they can replace habitual reactions with responses that serve them better. Being present also helps them not dwell on past events, such as times they've stuttered.

Evidence-based mindfulness strategies include:
- **Box breathing** (Fincham et al., 2023). Ask your patient to:
  - Breathe in through your nose as you slowly count to 4 in your head.
  - Hold your breath for a count of 4.
  - Exhale through your mouth for a count of 4.
  - Hold your breath again for a count of 4.
  - Repeat 3-4 rounds .
  - Take a few moments to rest, breathing in an easy manner
  - Continue on with your day, bringing this awareness of breath with you.
- **Body scan.** Ask your patient to:
  - Sit, stand, or lie down comfortably.
  - Take a few slow breaths, feeling your breath move through your body.
  - Feel the sensations in your forehead and then your jaw. Invite your body to relax into the breath.
  - Slowly work down the rest of your body, down to your fingertips and toes.
  - Take a few more moments to rest.
  - Continue on with your day, bringing this awareness of your body with you.

Acceptance and commitment therapy (ACT) uses mindfulness to improve self-acceptance and emotional regulation. **Cognitive behavioral therapy** paired with mindfulness can also enhance stuttering treatment (Gupta et al., 2016). Refer your patient to a qualified mental health professional for these treatments. In conjunction with speech therapy, ACT and cognitive behavioral therapy may decrease stuttering severity and social anxiety (Brignell et al., 2020; Menzies et al., 2019).

Desensitize Fears

The goal of this treatment isn't for your patient to stutter less in front of you. Instead, you and your patient will observe and learn how they usually communicate to desensitize their fears about their speech and stuttering. Start with a task and setting that are minimally stressful. Gradually add in factors that increase stress. These will differ from patient to patient.

When your patient stutters:
- Show that you notice the stutter, but you're not judging them for it.
- Immediately pause the task ("freeze") and have them deliberately prolong the disfluency.
- As they prolong the disfluency, ask them to change the pitch of the sound. Ask them to feel the tension in their body as they change the pitch. This will increase awareness of their body's reaction to phonating.

Managing avoidance behaviors

If your patient demonstrates avoidance behaviors, add in negative practice. Ask them to voluntarily stutter or pretend to stutter in an exaggerated manner. This can help desensitize emotions such as anxiety while stuttering.

Avoidance Reduction Therapy for Stuttering (ARTS®).

Avoidance Reduction Therapy is a well-established and evidence-based stuttering treatment. It aims to reduce fear and avoidance by addressing the emotional struggles a person goes through to avoid stuttering (Sisskin & Baer, 2016; The Stuttering Foundation, 2013). This treatment addresses avoidance behaviors (e.g., substituting words, closing eyes) and the feelings and attitudes that perpetuate the fear of stuttering. It was developed by Joseph and Vivian Sheehan, a psychologist and speech-language pathologist. You can learn how to do this treatment via in-person or online training courses.

Cognitive Restructuring

Cognitive restructuring is the process of identifying and changing ineffective beliefs. While speech therapy can help desensitize fears and promote mindfulness, it's best to refer out for cognitive restructuring treatment. A qualified mental health professional can use cognitive restructuring to treat social anxiety and activity limitations related to stuttering (Logan, 2020).

Promote Self-Disclosure

Self-disclosure is when your patient discloses that they stutter. Being open about stuttering improves self-esteem and quality of life (Boyle et al., 2018). Help them come up with a quick statement to share with unfamiliar listeners. For example, "I stutter," or "I'm a person who stutters, so if you hear pauses, that's what it is." Adding humor, a positive attitude, and confident body language can make self-disclosure more successful (Boyle, 2018).

Consider Support Groups

Being part of a supportive community can be a powerful experience for patients. Help them find local or online support groups for people who stutter.

How To Treat Neurogenic Stuttering

Neurogenic stuttering is a form of acquired stuttering caused by brain damage, most often after a stroke or TBI (Junuzovic-Zunic et al., 2021). It usually has a sudden onset and often co-occurs with other speech and/or language disorders, such as aphasia, apraxia, and dysarthria.

Neurogenic stuttering behaviors may include:
- Repetitions, prolongations, and blocks that are not restricted to initial sounds or syllables.
- Stuttering during automatic speech tasks, like counting.
- Not responding to fluency-inducing conditions (choral speaking, rhythmic speech, prolonged speech, singing, etc.; Manning & DiLollo, 2017).

People who have neurogenic stuttering are also less likely to have secondary behaviors like blinking or facial grimaces, which are common in childhood-onset stuttering. However, these may develop over time.

Neurogenic stuttering symptoms will improve as the underlying neurological problem improves. Many treatments that work for childhood-onset stuttering can also treat neurogenic stuttering.

Neurogenic stuttering treatments:
- Speech modification strategies
- Stuttering modification strategies (except fluency-inducing strategies)
- Negative reactions management

Speech therapy can also recommend ways to relax, such as mindfulness. You can also help patients overcome barriers to participation with tasks such as outings, phone calls, and strategies to overcome workplace challenges.

How To Treat Psychogenic Stuttering

Psychogenic stuttering is another form of acquired stuttering. It has a sudden onset and is caused by excessive stress (not a neurological disorder). However, psychogenic stuttering can co-occur with a neurological disorder.

Causes of psychogenic stuttering include:
- Trauma/PTSD
- Conversion disorder (real physical or sensory problems without a neurological cause)
- Adverse life events
- Psychological distress/exacerbation of a mental illness
- Drug dependence

Psychogenic stuttering behaviors may include:
- Repetitions, prolongations, and blocks in any position.
- Atypical fluency disruptions, like excessive repetitions of each phoneme.
- Worse symptoms on easier speaking tasks.
- Atypical secondary behaviors, such as an anxious body movement that's not related to the stutter.
- Unusual grammar.
- Rapid improvement of stuttering after disclosing emotionally sensitive information.

Psychogenic stuttering symptoms may resolve as your patient's stress resolves. Speech therapy can offer symptomatic treatment.

During treatment, be optimistic and encouraging. Avoid implying that a psychogenic stutter isn't valid or real. It may be helpful to frame the underlying cause of their stuttering as a positive prognostic factor as it means that full recovery is possible.

Psychogenic stuttering treatments:
- Speech modification and stuttering modification techniques.
- Helping identify and reduce muscle tension during speech.
- Practicing speech without tension.
- Normalizing prosody after fluency improves.
- Referring out for mental health counseling and stress reduction, as needed (Manning & DiLollo, 2017; Weightman, 2014).

Resonance

Resonance

Patients who can achieve velopharyngeal closure at least some of the time may benefit from speech therapy resonance treatment. With all resonance treatments, patient education is key. Teach patients about:

- The anatomy and physiology of the vocal tract
- Velopharyngeal movement and closure
- How nasals versus non-nasals are produced

Velopharyngeal Dysfunction Review

Velopharyngeal **insufficiency** is a **structural** issue. It's often secondary to cancer, traumatic injury, or lesions. There is insufficient (not enough) structure to achieve velopharyngeal closure. Refer these patients to specialists who can offer surgery or prosthetics.

Velopharyngeal **incompetence** is a **neurogenic** issue often related to dysarthria or oral apraxia. The structure is present but incompetent, which means it is ineffective in achieving velopharyngeal closure. Speech therapy can treat some cases of velopharyngeal incompetence.

Teamwork

Don't go it alone! Bring in the team if your patient needs support outside your scope of practice.

- Surgeon to address structural deficits, such as fistulas (Hutcheson & Lewin, 2013)
- Otolaryngologist to address other structural and functional issues
- Prosthodontist for palatal lift prosthesis or other prosthetics
- Primary care physician to treat underlying causes of swelling or inflammation in the nasal cavity (allergies, irritants causing hyponasality)
- Audiologist to manage suspected hearing loss causing hypernasality

Negative Practice

Once a patient can consistently say a phoneme with normal resonance, add negative practice. Negative practice is switching between normal and abnormal resonance on purpose. It can improve sensory awareness and help your patient feel more in control of their voice (Gillespie, n.d.)

How to use negative practice:

1. Ask your patient to describe how their "old" voice sounds and feels. Then, ask them to describe how their "new" voice sounds and feels.

2. They make up labels for their old and new voices. For example, "nasal voice" and "clear voice."

3. They say a target (reading paragraphs, conversation, etc.) using their "old" voice. Then, they switch to their "new" voice. Encourage them to feel the difference between the two.

4. Record both the normal and abnormal resonance production. Play it back for your patient to hear the difference.

Add negative practice whenever you think they would benefit from the extra feedback. For example, when they progress from monosyllabic words to bisyllabic words.

Hypernasality Treatment Options

Patients with hypernasality will sound more nasal. Their vowel sounds will be more nasal than is typical. For adults, common causes of hypernasality are spastic dysarthria, paralysis of some part of the vocal tract, myasthenia gravis, trauma to the velum, or even a habitual voice (Liu et al., 2022).

Only attempt treatment for hypernasality if your patient can achieve velopharyngeal closure—this means that their velum contacts the posterior pharyngeal wall. If they can achieve some closure, try intensive treatment (many sessions in a short period). If they show improvement during that time, then keep going. If not (or if they can't achieve closure), refer to a specialist for possible surgery, prosthetics, or orthodontics.

If your patient has some velar movement and hypernasality, try **stimulability testing** to see whether they can produce any sounds or words with more normal resonance. Model and use biofeedback as needed.

If your patient has dysarthria with subsequent hypernasality, treat with dysarthria strategies, like clear speech strategies.

Hypernasality techniques:
- Educate on resonance anatomy and physiology
- Start with vowels and /h/ plus a vowel
- If their hypernasality is severe, start with non-speech tasks like sighing or grunting
- Manipulate articulation, such as using wide-mouth postures
- Use biofeedback, such as feeling the vibrations in the nose when saying nasals vs. non-nasals
- Use ear training: They listen to voice recordings to become more aware of their resonance, especially the differences between nasal and non-nasal speech
- Train your patient to label their resonance, for example, "that was normal," or "that sounded hypernasal"
- Once they can achieve a more normal resonance, add in negative practice

(Stemple et al., 2018; Sapienza & Hoffman, 2020)

Hyponasality Treatment Options

Patients with hyponasality will sound like they have a head cold. Their vowels sound dampened. Acute hyponasality is often caused by a blockage along the nasal tract, such as tumors, nasal polyps, trauma, swelling due to allergies and congestion, or enlarged adenoids. Apraxia may also cause inconsistent resonance.

Behavioral speech therapy may be an option if your patient is stimulable for hyponasality strategies, but this is only after they've been assessed and treated by a specialist (for surgery, prosthetics, medications, etc.)

Hyponasality techniques:
- Educate on resonance anatomy and physiology
- Hum a prolonged /m/ and other nasals
- Feel vibrations in the nose
- Use biofeedback, such as a mirror fogging
- Exaggerate hypernasal resonance
- Reduce speech rate
- Use ear training: They listen to voice recordings to become more aware of their resonance
- Contrast how it feels in the face to make nasal vs oral sounds
- Once they can achieve a more normal resonance, add in negative practice

Provide immediate feedback, and ask your patient how it feels in their body to use nasal resonance. If they are stimulable for one or more strategies, gradually use them in more functional tasks (for example, transition from reading aloud to talking on the phone).

(Stemple et al., 2018)

Cul-de-sac Resonance Treatment Options

Patients with cul-de-sac resonance have voices that sound muffled or stuck in the back of the mouth. They may have dysarthria, small mouth opening, enlarged tonsils or adenoids, hearing loss, speak with a habitually retracted tongue posture, or have a new blockage such as nasal polyps (American Speech-Language-Hearing Association, n.d.k.)

The goal of these techniques is to promote a more anterior tongue position. Refer out if your patient has underlying medical issues such as enlarged tonsils. These should be managed before starting resonance treatment.

Ask your patient to try a technique and see if it improves communication effectiveness. If not, try a different technique.

Cul-de-sac resonance techniques:
- Educate on resonance anatomy and physiology
- Exaggerate mouth movements while speaking
- Use an extreme forward focus of the voice
- Use biofeedback by holding a hand in front of the mouth
- Use other feedback, such as listening to recordings of their voice
- Use ear training: They listen to voice recordings to become more aware of their resonance
- While doing speech tasks, keep the pitch the same while changing the loudness or speech rate
- Once they have a more normal resonance, add in negative practice

Provide immediate feedback, and ask your patient how it feels in their body to use nasal resonance. If they are stimulable for one or more strategies, gradually use them in more functional tasks (for example, transition from reading aloud to talking on the phone).

(Stemple et al., 2018; Sataloff, 2018)

Environmental Modifications

Improving the environment can help people with resonance disorders communicate more effectively.

- Choose a quiet space with minimal background noise.
- Make sure everyone can see each other's faces: turn on more lights, get closer, sit face-to-face.
- Address environmental allergies: take medications, use an air purifier, visit the doctor.
- Address side effects of cancer treatment such as dry mouth and tightness (sip water, use products with xylitol, jaw exercises and massage, etc.)
- Use video calls, like FaceTime or WhatsApp, instead of phone calls for the added visuals.
- Use the free Telecommunication Relay Services, where an operator helps people with communication disorders make phone calls (National Relay Service in Australia, Relay U.K. in the United Kingdom).

Prosthetics

Prosthetics are an option for patients with velopharyngeal insufficiency or incompetence that cannot be surgically corrected.

Prostheses can be uncomfortable and are only helpful if your patient is willing and remembers to wear them. If you believe that your patient may benefit from a prosthesis, educate them on its purpose, the pros and cons, and anatomy and physiology. If they understand and are willing, begin the referral process. You'll usually refer them to their primary care provider.

Palatal Lift Prosthesis.

A palatal lift prosthesis lifts the velum, allowing it to close against the posterior pharyngeal wall. It can improve intelligibility and even swallowing. Your patient may be a good candidate for a palatal lift prosthesis if they have **ALL** of the following:

- Velopharyngeal insufficiency with a large and consistent gap between the velum and posterior pharyngeal wall
- Relatively normal articulation: A palatal lift will only help with resonance. If your patient's articulation is poor, then a potentially uncomfortable lift may not be worth it for their communication
- Relatively intact respiration for speech
- Able to take care of the prosthesis and remember to use it
- Able to tolerate it
- Lack of gag reflex
- NO spasticity
- Unable or unwilling to have surgical correction

Your patient will usually starts with a temporary lift. Once they receive it, you can begin speech therapy. Help them get used to speaking as effectively as possible with the prosthesis. Over time, the prosthodontist may need to adjust the prosthesis to make it more comfortable and effective.

Obturators

Nasal obturators plug one or both nostrils to divert airflow from the nose to the mouth, which can improve intelligibility for some patients. Nasal obturators are made by an orthodontist, dentist, or plastic surgeon. Your patient may need a nasal obturator if a tooth extraction or orofacial surgery leaves a fistula or stoma that can't be corrected by surgery. They usually only wear it when they want to improve intelligibility, not all day long.

Palatal obturators look like dental retainers and are shaped to fill in fistulas in the palate. They're made by a prosthodontist. Your patient may need a palatal obturator if they have a fistula after tumor resection or trauma that can't be corrected by surgery. Patients usually wear them while speaking and eating.

Speech bulbs look like elongated dental retainers. They act as velum extensions to achieve velopharyngeal closure and may be combined with a palatal obturator. Speech bulbs are made by a prosthodontist. Your patient may need a speech bulb after a resection, trauma, or history of a repaired cleft that shortened the velum and can't be corrected by surgery. Patients usually wear them while speaking and eating.

Forward Focus Strategies

Forward focus means using a voice that resonates forward, towards the front of the face. This strategy is used in voice therapy but can also be helpful for some resonance disorders, including hyper- or hyponasality due to incomplete glottal closure related to presbylaryngsis, vocal nodules, polyps, or edema.

Teach patients how to tell that they're speaking with a forward focus by feeling the vibrations in the front of their faces (nose, lips, and/or mouth). This improved awareness can help them self-correct and remember to use their strategies.

Forward focus protocol (Stemple et al., 2018):
1. Start with education. Explain the difference between back-focus and front (forward)-focus.
2. Do simple non-speech tasks that promote forward focus, like buzzing the lips ("motorcycle noises") and trilling the tongue on the alveolar ridge.
    - Or wrap a comb in wax paper. Your patient will place the comb between their lips and hum or buzz their lips.
3. Hum, using a tight, constricted back focus.
4. Hum with a breathy focus.
5. Hum with a very front, almost nasal focus.
6. Chant CV and VC nasal syllables, like "ma ma ma" and "um um um." Chant slowly and softly, using a slightly higher pitch than usual. Feel the voice in the front of the face.
7. Do ear training. Help your patient listen to and identify the difference between a nasal versus non-nasal voice.
8. Use negative practice. For example, chant using their old, poorly focused voice. Then, switch back to the more resonant, forward-focused voice.
9. Say phrases using a variety of speeds and loudnesses. Start very slowly and softly, increase to fast and loud, and gradually slow down again.
10. Say phrases in an exaggerated, sing-songy voice.
11. Use negative practice again. For example, say phrases using their old, poorly focused voice. Then, switch back to the more resonant, forward-focused voice.
12. Continue using forward focus and negative practice with sentences, paragraphs, monologues, and conversation.

Voice

Voice

Behavioral voice treatment can help patients speak with a clear, easy, and healthy voice. With all voice treatments, patient education is key. Educate on the anatomy and physiology of normal voice production vs. their current voice production. Describe how the treatment options you chose can help. Help them identify their own vocal quality using biofeedback and ear training. Use audio or video recordings (with the proper permissions), then review the before-and-after recordings with your patient to show how the treatment is improving their voice.

Some patients need medication and/or surgery to manage their voice disorder. Examples are reflux medication for severe GERD or injections or surgery for vocal fold paralysis. Refer to a specialist as needed.

Voice treatment options can be divided into 4 categories. This chapter will cover each:
- Vocal hygiene
- Symptomatic voice therapy
- Physiologic voice therapy
- Psychogenic voice therapy

Teamwork
Don't go it alone! Bring in the team if your patient needs support outside your scope of practice.
- Otolaryngologists for instrumental assessment and treatment of laryngeal disorders (American Speech-Language-Hearing Association, n.d.a.)
- Physician or pharmacist for pharmacological management (allergy medications, etc.)
- Surgeon for management of anatomical or physiological issues related to the vocal folds
- Mental health professional to address mental health needs

Vocal Tension or Hyperfunctioning Treatment

Use one or more of the following treatment options if your patient has vocal tension or a hyperfunctioning voice.

- Semi-occluded Vocal Tract Exercises, including lip trills
- Resonant Voice Therapy (Watts & Awan, 2019)
- Conversation Training Therapy
- Vocal Function Exercises
- Accent Method
- Forward Focus Strategies
- Flow Phonation
- Manual Circumlaryngeal Massage (Dehqan & Scherer, 2019)
- Speaking with the tongue slightly forward to open the larynx
- Nonspeech tasks like throat clearing, grunting, inhalation phonation, and coughing for severe tension
- Chewing
- Yawn-sigh (Boone & McFarlane, 1993)
- Confidential voice (American Speech-Language-Hearing Association, n.d.a.)
- Inhalation phonation
- Amplification to avoid hyperfunctioning
- Progressive muscle relaxation
- Deep breathing
- Stretches for the head and neck

Vocal Weakness or Hypofunctioning Treatment

Vocal hypofunctioning is often related to glottal incompetence, which can cause a breathy, quiet voice. Paradoxically, glottal hypofunctioning can cause hyperfunctioning in other parts of the vocal tract as the body overcompensates for weak muscles, which can lead to strain and a hoarse vocal quality. Check to see how your patient's muscles are functioning with a referral for instrumental assessment (i.e. stroboscopy) with an otolaryngologist or other voice specialist.

Use one or more of the following options to help treat your patient's vocal weakness or hypofunctioning voice.

- LSVT LOUD (LSVT Global, 2022)
- Respiratory Muscle Strength Training, including EMST and IMST (Desjardins & Bonilha, 2020; Pitts et al., 2009)
- Resonant Voice Therapy
- Vocal Function Exercises
- SPEAK OUT!
- Phonation Resistance Training Exercises
- Digital manipulation for unilateral vocal fold paralysis
- Chant Speech
- Twang vocal quality (American Speech-Language-Hearing Association, n.d.a.)
- Hard glottal attack (Watts & Awan, 2019)
- Half swallow boom, but be aware of contraindications such as high blood pressure
- Nonspeech tasks such as pushing and pulling hard on a surface to help achieve glottal closure
- Amplification to increase loudness

Essential Vocal Tremor Strategies

Essential vocal tremor is a neurologic condition where the voice sounds tremulous, especially with increased vocal effort. Tremors can occur in the larynx, tongue, jaw, face, head, or respiratory system. Here are some essential vocal tremor treatments:

- Yawn sigh (Boone & McFarlane, 1993)
- Easy onsets
- Forward focus
- Open throat
- Slightly higher pitch
- Relaxation and breathing exercises
- Slightly faster speech rate

Breathy Voice Strategies

Try these strategies with patients who have a quiet, breathy voice:

.

- Take more frequent and deeper breaths to increase lung volume and lung recoil
- Reduce speaking rate to preserve breath support
- Talk louder
- Use a twangy voice. This can make their voice louder with less effort. The goal is increased vocal efficiency (Lombard & Steinhauer, 2007)
- Use hard glottal attacks or pushing for moderate to severe breathiness. **Use only for a short time** as these strategies may cause unwanted tightness or damage
- Use ear training. Help your patient identify when they're breathy so that they can use their techniques
- Use pursed-lip breathing for patients who have COPD. This can improve ventilation and release air trapped in the lungs while reducing effort (Sapienza & Hoffman, 2020)

Vocal Hygiene

Vocal hygiene aims to help patients do less damaging vocal behaviors while adding healthier behaviors. Here is a vocal hygiene protocol.

Find the cause. First, identify the key underlying behaviors causing the voice disorder. For example, poor breath support causing vocal strain.

Educate. Include visual aids to describe how these damaging behaviors affect their vocal anatomy/physiology.

Find triggers. Identify when and why the damaging behaviors occur, such as being in a specific environment, at the end of the day, or when they're stressed.

Improve self-awareness. Identify damaging behaviors when they occur in the treatment session. Teach strategies to increase awareness and encourage carryover outside of the session.

Add healthy behaviors. Introduce healthy behaviors to replace or modify the damaging ones. For example, use breath support, drink water instead of caffeine, and use a humidifier if in a dry climate. Practice strategies in a variety of speaking settings to encourage carryover.

An important vocal hygiene behavior is to hydrate, although this can be hard for patients to adhere to. Educate about why hydration is important for vocal health and how to do it. For example:
- Being hydrated means having thin mucus, which is healthy for your vocal folds. If you're not hydrated, your mucus gets stickier and can disrupt normal vocal fold vibration.
- Drink even more water if you do extra physical activity or if you drink caffeine.

Symptomatic Voice Therapy

As the name suggests, these voice therapy options treat voice symptoms (Stemple & Klaben, 2018), such as abnormal vocal quality, reduced loudness, or lowered pitch.

Experiment to determine which options work best for each patient. Stick with the few that help your patient produce a cleaner, more effortless voice.

With doing symptomatic voice therapy, use a hierarchy of tasks. For example, start with single phonemes such as /m/ or /a/, then progress to CV words, single words, phrases, etc., until your patient can have a conversation using a clean, easy voice.

Chant speech
Chant speech treats vocal fatigue and vocal tension. Ask your patient to use a monotone voice, easy onsets, and equal stress. This helps create a forward focus while reducing vocal tension. While effective, chant speak can sound funny when doing it! It can help to have a sense of humor about it.

Confidential voice
This strategy treats vocal tension. Ask your patient to use a breathy, quiet, and easy voice without whispering. It's often only used temporarily, such as after a vocal surgery or vocal injury.

Inhalation phonation
This is a treatment for ventricular phonation, functional aphonia, or muscle tension dysphonia (American Speech-Language-Hearing Association, n.d.a.) Inhalation phonation can offload tension from the ventricular folds. First, ask your patient to slowly breathe in and out with an open mouth. Then, ask them to say a high-pitched (American Speech-Language-Hearing Association, n.d.a.) sound while inhaling.

Once they get the hang of it, ask them to also say the sound on the exhale. For example, they say "ahh" on the inhale and the exhale of the same breath. Once they can consistently and easily produce a vowel sound on the exhale, work up to longer utterances on the exhale only.

Supportive posture

A supportive posture improves respiratory support for speech. Encourage your patient to sit comfortably upright. They should align their neck and spine, relax their upper body, and face the listener (Stemple, n.d.)

Relaxation and stretching

These treat vocal tension and effortful phonation. Progressive muscle relaxation, deep breathing, and visualization of relaxing scenes facilitate relaxation (American Speech-Language-Hearing Association, n.d.a.) To relieve tension, teach head and neck stretches.

Chewing

This strategy can increase oral resonance and reduce laryngeal and vocal tension. Ask your patient to pretend they're chewing food while exaggerating their jaw and tongue movements. When they can chew in a relaxed manner, ask them to say "uhhh" while chewing. They will work up to saying words and phrases while chewing and continue to monitor that their larynx feels relaxed. As your patient says longer phrases, phase out chewing.

Biofeedback

Biofeedback helps patients increase awareness of and make changes to their 'vocal pitch, loudness, quality, and effort" (American Speech-Language-Hearing Association, n.d.a.). Biofeedback can be auditory, visual, or kinesthetic. Auditory biofeedback may involve recording their voice. Visual biofeedback may include watching a sound level meter as they speak. Kinesthetic feedback may be feeling tightened abs and relaxed shoulders when they speak loudly.

Rate and rhythm

Teach patients to add pauses and to prolong vowel sounds to reduce speech rate and increase intelligibility.

Amplification

Use a personal amplifier to make the voice louder without the extra effort. Amplifiers can be handy in loud or social settings, such as having lunch with friends at a cafe.

Semi-Occluded Vocal Tract (SOVT) Exercises

SOVT treats vocal hyperfunction (Rosenberg, 2014). A semi-occluded vocal tract takes pressure off the vocal folds and onto the front of the face by partially occluding (rounding) the lips. This reduces vocal fold tension to create an easier and clearer voice.

The patient will focus on feeling the vibrations of a forward and resonant voice at the lips or tongue while keeping an open throat. The goal is usually measured in dB loudness.

SOVT exercises and approaches aim to help patients feel a forward and resonant voice and open throat to say words, phrases, sentences, paragraphs, and conversation. Several voice treatments incorporate SOVT exercises, including Vocal Function Exercises, Resonant Voice Therapy, and the Accent Method. However, you can also use SOVT exercises on their own.

SOVT exercises. Encourage an easy, forward focus. Ask your patient to feel the vibrations at their lips and to have an open throat.
1. Hum
2. Sustain then glide high to low to high 3 times on the following:
    - Voiced fricatives /v,th,z/
    - Trilling the tongue
    - Trilling the lips
    - Nasals
    - /u,i/
3. Speak through a straw or kazoo. Encourage a lot of intonation!
4. Sing while reading phrases and sentences.
5. Buzz the lips or do tongue trills.
    - If a patient can't sustain a lip or tongue trill (Rosenberg, 2014) they can use a small card or sticky note. Hold the card perpendicular to the lips and ask them to glide up and down in a comfortable range.

Diaphragmatic Breathing

Voice disorders can involve breath strength and control. Dysphonia may cause a weak, breathy, hoarse, strangled, or rough vocal quality due to reduced breath support (American Speech-Language-Hearing Association, n.d.a.)

Your patient may benefit from breath support exercise if they have any of the following:
- Functional voice disorders, including:
  - Vocal tension/hoarseness
  - Vocal fatigue
  - Muscle tension dysphonia
  - Phonotrauma
  - Ventricular phonation
  - Phonation breaks
  - Asthenia (weak voice)
- Structural voice disorders, including vocal nodules or glottal stenosis
- Neurological voice disorders, including:
  - Parkinson's disease
  - Multiple sclerosis
  - Pseudobulbar palsy
  - Recurrent laryngeal nerve paralysis
  - Adductor/abductor spasmodic dysphonia

As your patients build up their breath support, have them progress to voiceless sounds, then vowels, then sentences, and so on.

Diaphragmatic breathing protocol:
- Ask your patient to place one hand on the stomach and the other hand on the chest.
- They'll take a deep breath into the diaphragm
  - "As you breathe in, feel your stomach go out and chest remain more still. As you breathe out, feel your stomach pull in and chest remain still."
- Add voiceless sounds, like /h/ and /s/, while diaphragmatic breathing. They will hold each sound out for as long as they can.
- Gradually work up to vowel sounds while diaphragmatic breathing, holding each sound out.
- Work up to single words, then longer words, phrases, and sentences while diaphragmatic breathing.

Accent Method

The accent method of voice therapy, developed by Svend Smith, focuses on abdominal breathing and prosody to reduce tension and create an easier, more robust voice. The "accent" refers to an emphasized beat you'd see in sheet music (not a difference in pronunciation). It also focuses on timing to help develop new motor programs. The accent method can improve sound pressure level and fundamental frequency (Kotby et al., 1993). You can purchase an instruction manual written by the developers online.

Here's an example of how to do the accent method:
Throughout treatment, focus on having the power of their voice coming from their abdomen.

1. Your patient lies down or leans back.
2. They place a hand on their stomach as they practice diaphragmatic (abdominal) breathing. They focus on feeling the connection between their stomach movements and their breath movements.
3. They say voiceless fricatives, sustaining each for a short time while focusing on the effort coming from the abdomen.
     ○ For example, "fff" and "sss."
4. They sit up.
5. They say a voiceless fricative softly for two seconds. Then repeat that sound with more strength. In other words, they will put an 'accent' on the second repetition by pulling the abdomen in more forcefully to make the stronger sound. Repeat with other voiceless fricatives.
     ○ For example, "ssss SSSSSSSS."
6. They repeat this in different postures (stand, sway, walk, etc.)
7. They sit back down.
8. They use a soft, breathy voice to say voiced phonemes and CV syllables with a slow tempo. The first repetition will be weaker, and the second will be stronger. Again, they will put an 'accent' on the second repetition by pulling the abdomen in more forcefully to make the stronger sound.
     ○ For example, "woooo WOOOO," "jjjj JJJJJ," "zzzz ZZZZ"
9. Then, they say voiced phonemes and CV syllables using a variety of tempos, loudness, and pitches.
     ○ For example, "yeah yeah YEAH YEAH YEAH YEAH."
10. To help generalize, your patient uses this rhythm with repetition, reading, and then conversation.

Conversation Training Therapy

Conversation training therapy (CTT) is a treatment for benign vocal fold lesions and muscle tension dysphonia (Gillespie et al., 2019). It uses conversation as the only stimulus so that voice therapy gains will generalize outside of treatment (Gartner-Schmidt et al., 2016). CTT can help produce a healthier voice, reduce voice handicap index scores, increase voice awareness, and improve vocal efficiency. It was developed by Jackie Gartner-Schmidt and Amanda Gillespie.

The primary technique of CTT is clear speech. Throughout treatment, your patient practices clear speech in conversations on topics of their choosing. The clinician models and cues as needed. The goal is articulatory precision (Gartner-Schmidt, n.d.)

Tenants of Conversation Training Therapy

1. Focus on clear speech and articulatory precision.

2. Build rapport! Encourage patients to set their own goals and to choose the topics of conversation.

3. Increase auditory and kinesthetic awareness. Train patients to compare their old voice to their new voice. Have them feel and hear their new voice vs their old voice. Use ear training, auditory feedback, and kinesthetic feedback to do this.

4. Use negative practice. Occasionally have your patient use their old, unhealthy voice and compare it to their new, healthy voice. This will improve their auditory and kinesthetic awareness and empower them to know that they're in control of their voice.

5. Use "basic training gestures." Sprinkle in these simple voice tasks throughout a session to remind your patient what an easy voice feels like. Basic training gestures include lip buzz, lip trills, tongue trills, CVC nasal words like "molm," and extreme forward focus.

6. Vary prosody. Teach how to improve pitch, loudness, and rhythm.

Expiratory Muscle Strength Training

Expiratory muscle strength training (EMST) treats respiratory weaknesses and dysphonia. It can improve respiratory muscle strength and the coordination of respiration, phonation, and resonance for a healthier voice (Desjardins & Bonilha, 2020; Pitts et al., 2009).

EMST follows a protocol and uses a handheld device into which a patient forcefully exhales. The device offers resistance that allows airflow only once the patient hits a set threshold of effort. Training is available online.

General EMST protocol:

1. Measure your patient's maximum expiratory pressure (MEP) using a respiratory pressure meter.

2. Set the EMST device (e.g. EMST 150) to the recommended MEP percentage (e.g. 70-75% of MEP).

3. Instruct your patient to use the EMST device:
   - Plug your nose/use a nose plug to prevent air loss through the nose as needed.
   - Take a deep breath and hold it briefly.
   - Place the device behind your teeth with your lips tight around the mouthpiece.
   - Blow forcefully through the device. Hold your cheeks with your free hand to maintain a tight seal if needed.
   - Rest 15-30 seconds before repeating.
   - Repeat around 5 repetitions, 5 times per day (25 reps total), 5 days per week, for around 4 weeks. The number of repetitions and level of resistance will depend on each patient. Follow the referring provider's instructions.

4. You may also recommend a maintenance program when the main program is completed.

Inspiratory Muscle Strength Training

Inspiratory muscle strength training (IMST) is an exercise program that can improve respiratory muscle strength and vocal quality in some people with voice disorders (Desjardins & Bonilha, 2020; Desjardins et al., 2022). IMST follows a protocol and uses a handheld device that offers resistance when the patient inhales forcefully into it.

General IMST protocol:

1. Set the IMST device (e.g. POWERbreathe) to the recommended resistance level.

2. Instruct your patient to use the device:
   - Sit upright.
   - Plug your nose/use a nose plug to prevent air loss through the nose if needed.
   - Place the IMST mouthpiece in your mouth. Create a strong seal.
   - Breathe out as much air as you can, then take a fast, forceful breath in through your mouth. Inhale as much air as you can as fast as you can.
   - Breathe out slowly and with minimal effort until you're out of breath. Let your shoulders relax. If you feel lightheaded, slow down and pause.
   - Pause. Take another fast, forceful breath in, then breathe out slowly. Repeat as recommended.

The number of repetitions and level of resistance will depend on each patient. Follow the referring provider's instructions.

Incentive Spirometry

An incentive spirometer is a device that can improve lung health. It helps patients take slow, deep breaths and clear secretions from the lungs, which is important when recovering from certain lung diseases and surgeries. If your patient received an incentive spirometer from their physician, respiratory therapist, or other professional, you may choose to incorporate it into treatment.

General incentive spirometry protocol:

1. Set the incentive spirometer at the recommended target.

2. Breathe all the way out, then place the mouthpiece between the lips.

3. Breathe in deeply through the mouth.
   - Watch the flow rate guide rise to hit the target.
   - Continue breathing in for as long as you can (or as long as instructed by the doctor or respiratory therapist).

4. Breathe out slowly and take a short rest.

5. Repeat per physician or respiratory therapist recommendations

Check with the physician first if your patient has a respiratory tract infection, uncontrolled hypertension, dementia, or other potential contraindications (Franklin & Anjum, 2023).

Resonant Voice Therapy

Resonant Voice Therapy may improve vocal quality in people with muscle tension dysphonia, vocal cord nodules, and even vocal fold paralysis (Kao et al., 2017; Liu et al., 2022; Verdolini-Marston et al., 1995; Verdolini Abbott et al., 2012; Watts et al., 2019; Yiu et al., 2017).

Resonant voice therapy aims to create a strong, clean, healthy voice that takes tension off the vocal folds. You'll teach patients to speak with a forward focus while feeling the voice at the front of the face. This may feel like a buzz or vibration in the alveolar ridge, nose, teeth, lips, and facial bones. You can learn Lessac-Madsen Resonant Voice Therapy in their 4-week training program.

General resonant voice therapy protocol:

1. Your patient sighs from a high to low pitch while saying "molm." Encourage them to use a forward-focus voice. Repeat.

2. Repeat the word "molm" over and over on a musical note that's slightly higher than their conversational tone:
   - First, they'll repeat the word and vary the speed of the repetitions
   - Then, they'll repeat the word while varying how broad or narrow the vibrational output of each repetition is.
   - Next, they'll repeat the word while varying speed and loudness.
   - Finally, they'll repeat the word using speech-like prosody.

3. Chant /m/ heavy sentences on a musical note:
   - First, encourage them to overarticulate their mouth movements while saying the sentences.
   - Then, ask them to use speech-like prosody.

4. Repeat "mamapapa" on a musical note equal to their habitual conversational pitch:
   - First, they'll repeat "mamapapa" while varying the speed of repetitions.
   - Then, they'll repeat "mamapapa" while varying the speed and loudness of the repetitions.
   - Finally, they'll repeat "mamapapa" using speech-like prosody.

5. Chant sentences with /m/ and /p/ on a musical note equal to their habitual conversational pitch:
   - First, they'll chant and overarticulate mouth movements.
   - Then, they'll chant and use an exaggerated prosody.

6. Chant sentences with 5-7 syllables on a musical note equal to their habitual conversational pitch:
   - First, they'll overarticulate the mouth movements and use exaggerated prosody while chanting the sentences.
   - Then, they'll use a more natural way of speaking while maintaining a forward focus.

7. Read a paragraph over and over:
   - Pause only to take a breath; otherwise, keep reading. Encourage using a forward focus.
   - Then, ask them to gradually use a more natural way of speaking, pausing at natural times.

8. Have a conversation about something interesting and familiar to your patient.
   - Continue to encourage them to use a forward focus while speaking.

9. Speak using a forward focus in everyday settings. Start with a controlled setting, then increase the challenge, such as talking in a noisy room.

10. Finally, have conversations that elicit strong emotions, such as hilarity, anger, sadness, or happiness.

Lee Silverman Voice Treatment

LSVT LOUD (LSVT LOUD) is an evidence-based voice treatment program for patients with Parkinson's disease and other neurological conditions. Its goal and focus are to improve vocal loudness. It teaches patients to think loud, work hard, and recalibrate what their "normal" voice is.

LSVT LOUD has an intensive schedule of 16 1-hour treatment sessions (4 sessions per week for 4 weeks), plus daily homework. LSVT-X is an option for patients who can only do 2 sessions per week.

LSVT was developed by Lorraine Ramig. You can get trained and certified on the LSVT LOUD website.

Main components of LSVT LOUD treatment:

1. Your patient sustains "ah" using a loud voice for as long as they can. Repeat a set number of times:
   - First, in their habitual pitch.
   - Then, at their highest comfortable pitch.
   - Finally, at their lowest comfortable pitch.

2. They read a list of functional phrases over and over using a loud voice.

3. They complete other drills, such as reading paragraphs aloud or having a conversation using a loud voice.

4. They complete daily homework, which include drills from in-session practice and a carryover assignment (e.g. ordering coffee at their favorite cafe while thinking loud).

SPEAK OUT!

SPEAK OUT! is a voice treatment program developed by the Parkinson's Voice Project. It aims to help people with Parkinson's disease produce a stronger, clearer voice by teaching them to speak with intent. Treatment consists of 8-12 speech therapy sessions that are 30-45 minutes long plus twice-daily homework.

The program offers many supports, including weekly groups and extensive follow-up. You can learn how to do this treatment on the SPEAKOUT! website (Parkinson Voice Project, n.d.)

Main components of SPEAK OUT! treatment (Sullivan et al., 2024; Watts, 2016; Reid Health, n.d.):
- Vocal warm-up
- Vowel prolongation exercises
- Gliding and intonation exercises
- Automatic sequences, such as counting
- Reading aloud sentences to paragraphs of gradually increasing length and complexity
- Cognitive tasks, such as discussing needed items for different scenarios

Flow Phonation

Flow Phonation is a voice treatment for muscle tension dysphonia/aphonia in people who hold back airflow. Flow phonation attempts to target all speech subsystems at one time with the goal of eventually speaking using a normal, easy voice (Watts et al., 2015). Flow phonation was modified from "stretch and flow phonation" by Jackie Gartner-Schmidt. You can learn more about this treatment by taking her online course.

General flow phonation protocol (Gartner-Schmidt, n.d.):
The patient will focus on feeling forward airflow without throat tightness throughout treatment. Also, emphasize that they focus on feeling the sounds of speech.

1. Release airflow without voicing with a sigh on /u/ (rounded lips).
   o Hold a tissue in front of the lips for biofeedback.

2. Next, move on to articulated airflow. As the patient releases voiceless airflow, they will slowly move their articulators.

3. Add voicing to airflow. Release a sigh on /u/, then add in the voice. Move from voiceless fricatives to voiced fricatives, for example, /s/ to /z/.

4. Add articulation to this voicing and airflow.

5. Practice discriminating between breathy voice, flow voice, and pressed phonation. Feel and hear the difference between each.

6. Next, practice articulatory precision with words, phrases, and sentences.

Phonation Resistance Training Exercises

PhoRTE® (pronounced "forte") uses high-intensity vocal exercise to help patients with presbylaryngis produce a stronger voice. You can learn how to do this treatment on the PhoRTE website.

General components of PhoRTE treatment (Stemple et al., 2018):

1. Your patient starts by saying /a/ in a strong voice for as long as possible, repeating it 10 times.

2. Then, they glide on /a/ from low to high to low in a strong voice, repeating 5 times.

3. They glide on /a/ from high to low to high, repeating 5 times.

4. They read 10 functional phrases in a loud, higher-pitched voice and then in a loud, lower-pitched voice.

5. They say a 2-minute monologue with a strong voice, as if they were in a noisy public space such as a cafe.

Vocal Function Exercises

Vocal function exercises (VFE) is a treatment program that brands itself as "physical therapy for the vocal cords" (Stemple et al., 2018). VFE balances respiration, phonation, and resonance to improve and protect against voice problems (Angadi et al., 2019). VFE has 4 exercises practiced daily throughout an 8-10 week program. Patient also complete a prescriptive home program. Measure progress by your patient's maximum phonation time.

Joseph Stemple teaches the VFE in resources published by Plural Publishing, Inc., and an online continuing education course on Medbridge.

Overview of the 4 vocal function exercises (Stemple, n.d.):
Throughout treatment, the patient focuses on using a forward focus while keeping an open throat and rounded lips ("reversed megaphone").

1. **Warm up.** Your patient uses an extreme forward-focused, soft voice while saying "eee" for as long as they can on a specific musical note.

2. **Stretch.** They glide up from their lowest comfortable sound to their highest comfortable sound on the word "knoll" (nasal initial with liquid final).

3. **Contract.** Repeat step 2, but they glide down from the highest comfortable sound to the lowest comfortable sound on "knoll".

4. **Power.** They say "knoll" without the initial nasal for as long as possible on a series of musical notes.
   - Progress to phrases, sentences, then conversation.

Psychogenic Voice Therapy

Psychogenic voice therapy options treat voice disorders caused by underlying psychosocial or emotional reasons, such as dysphonia caused by anxiety.

Psychogenic voice therapy may include (Stemple et al., 2018):
- Listening about your patient's current or recent stressors and providing counseling. Refer to a mental health professional as needed.
- Educating on how stress affects the voice, the vocal folds, and other structures in the throat.
- Helping reduce tension.
- Completing non-speech tasks to elicit a voice, such as throat clearing, coughing, sighing, gargling, or laughing.
- Encouraging lifestyle changes, such as decreasing smoking, throat-clearing, and caffeine intake.

Biofeedback

Biofeedback allows your patient to see, hear, and/or feel their voice. Their helps your patient become more aware of how their voice is functioning in the moment, which can cue them to use their voice strategies.

Feel voice vibrations

Encourage your patient to feel vibrations in the front of their face, like their lips and the tip of their nose. If they can't feel these vibrations, their voice may be tense, or they may not be using a forward-focus.

If they can't feel the vibrations in the front of their face, ask them to hum or project their voice outward. Next, ask them to say "ahh" and then their name while feeling that buzz in the front of their face.

See and feel the breath

If your patient tends to hold their breath or have a lot of tension when they speak, ask them to use a breathy voice. They can hold a tissue, their hand, or a small mirror in front of their nose and mouth to feel and/or see their breath.

The goal is to learn what a healthy voice feels like inside their body. Once they can do that, they won't need to hold anything in front of their face.

Listen to the voice

Record them speaking in their normal voice (after getting proper permissions). Ask them to listen to the recording, then ask, "How easy or hard is t to understand what you're saying? How fast do you speak? How does your voice sound in general?"

Next, record them talking while using their speech strategies. Together, Compare it to the first recording.

See-Scape™

This device provides visual feedback of nasal air emissions caused by velopharyngeal incompetence. Your patient inserts the nasal tip into their nose, and if air emissions occur as they speak, a float rises to the middle of a plastic tube. See-Scape is available for purchase online.

Nasometer

A nasometer is an instrument that provides visual feedback of nasalence. It can evaluate and treat resonance disorders caused by velopharyngeal dysfunction. The device measures whether too much or too little sound comes from a patient's nose during speech. It's available for purchase from medical retailers.

Oral and Nasal Listener™

The Oral and Nasal Listener is essentially a stethoscope with a funnel that your patient speaks into. It amplifies nasal sounds, giving patients auditory feedback on the difference between nasal and non-nasal sounds. It comes with additional tubing that allows the clinician to listen in simultaneously. It's available for purchase from Super Duper® Publications.

Stethoscope

Place the stethoscope on the side of your patient's nose. Ask them to repeat or read material loaded with non-nasals. They shouldn't hear breathing as they speak. If they do, introduce hypernasality strategies.

Unilateral Vocal Fold Paralysis Treatment

Behavioral speech therapy can help some cases of unilateral vocal fold paralysis. Treatment may restore some voice and prevent maladaptive behaviors such as hyperfunctioning.

Paralysis with no known underlying cause (idiopathic paralysis) may spontaneously recover within a year of onset. In these cases, a surgery referral should be delayed to monitor for improvements (Stemple et al., 2018). The patient may still receive injections to help with medialization, as needed.

The goal of behavioral speech therapy is to reposition the vocal folds. It aims to strengthen the non-paralyzed vocal fold enough to cross the midline and improve vocal quality. However, it's important to find the balance between producing voice and not causing hyper-functioning.

The following treatments are short term. Use them for a few weeks at most. These are NOT a long-term solution. If your patient shows no improvement in voice production, stop these exercises and refer to a voice specialist or surgeon.

Head Turn
Ask your patient to slowly turn their head to the affected side while saying prolonged vowels. If vocal quality improves with the head turn, have them say a list of words and then phrases. Identify which head position provides the greatest change in vocal quality.

Hard Glottal Attack

Week 1: Ask your patient to build up air pressure, then say the following:

1. "ah ah"
2. "eee eee"
3. "eye eye"
4. "oh oh"
5. "ooh ooh"
6. "ought ought"
7. "eat eat"
8. "I'm I'm"
9. "oat oat"
10. "oot oot"

Week 2: Ask them to build up air pressure, then say the vowel sounds (above) while gliding down to a lower pitch.

Week 3: Finally, ask your patient to build up air pressure AND do an isometric push (press palms together, pull up on a chair, etc.). They then say the vowel sounds while gliding down to a lower pitch. They release the push as soon as they finish speaking.

Manual Therapy Techniques for Vocal Tension

Manual therapy is a modality often used in physical therapy that involves using your hands to provide treatment. Use it to treat patients with laryngeal tension that's causing laryngeal elevation. Manual therapy for vocal tension uses massage-like movements to relax and reposition the larynx and surrounding structures (Stemple et al., 2018). Add other relaxation techniques and mental health referrals as needed.

Amount of pressure to use. Start by applying slightly more pressure than you would for laryngeal palpation during a swallowing assessment. You're working close to the carotid artery, so apply enough pressure to be effective—without knocking your patient out! Increase pressure gradually, be mindful of your finger placement, and monitor your patient's comfort level.

How to find major structures. To find the major structures, start with laryngeal palpation. Ask your patient to swallow their saliva to find their thyroid prominence (Adam's apple). From there, find the thyroid notch and hyoid bone. Practice finding these structures on yourself and willing loved ones to increase confidence. If you still feel unsure, ask your workplace for more training.

Hyoid Pushback

1. Use your pointer finger and lay it against your patient's throat, just above the hyoid bone.
    - Apply inward and downward pressure as your patient says, "ahhh."
    - Slightly change the amount of pressure you apply inward and downward to see whether it changes their vocal quality.
2. Repeat with your finger on the hyoid.
3. Repeat with your finger just below the hyoid.

Note the placement, direction, and amount of pressure that improves your patient's pitch, loudness, and/or vocal quality. Teach them to use sensory feedback and negative practice to feel the difference between a tense and relaxed voice.

Thyroid Pulldown

1. Place your thumb and pointer finger on each superior cornu of the thyroid cartilage.
2. Apply downward pressure as your patient says, "ahhh."

Note the placement and amount of pressure that improves your patient's pitch, loudness, and/or vocal quality. Teach them to use sensory feedback and negative practice to feel the difference between a tense and relaxed voice.

Circumlaryngeal Massage

Use circumlaryngeal massage to treat functional dysphonia and aphonia. It can stretch and relax muscle tissue and fascia, increase circulation, and reduce pain and discomfort. Your patient will hum as you massage. Listen for changes in vocal pitch, loudness, and/or quality.

How to do manual circumlaryngeal massage:
1. Place your thumb and pointer finger on either side of the hyoid bone.
   - Apply pressure with a slight circular motion, moving back toward each greater horn of the hyoid bone as your patient hums.
   - Move the hyoid bone laterally, slowly and gently moving it slightly from side to side as your patient hums.
2. Repeat, applying pressure with a slight circular motion, starting on either side of the thyroid notch. Your patient continues to hum.
3. Repeat, starting on each posterior border of the thyroid cartilage.
4. Place your thumb and pointer finger on the superior border of the thyroid cartilage.
   - Apply pressure down toward the inferior border as your patient hums.
   - Move the thyroid cartilage laterally as your patient hums.

Note the placement and amount of pressure that improves your patient's voice (vocal quality, effort, and range).

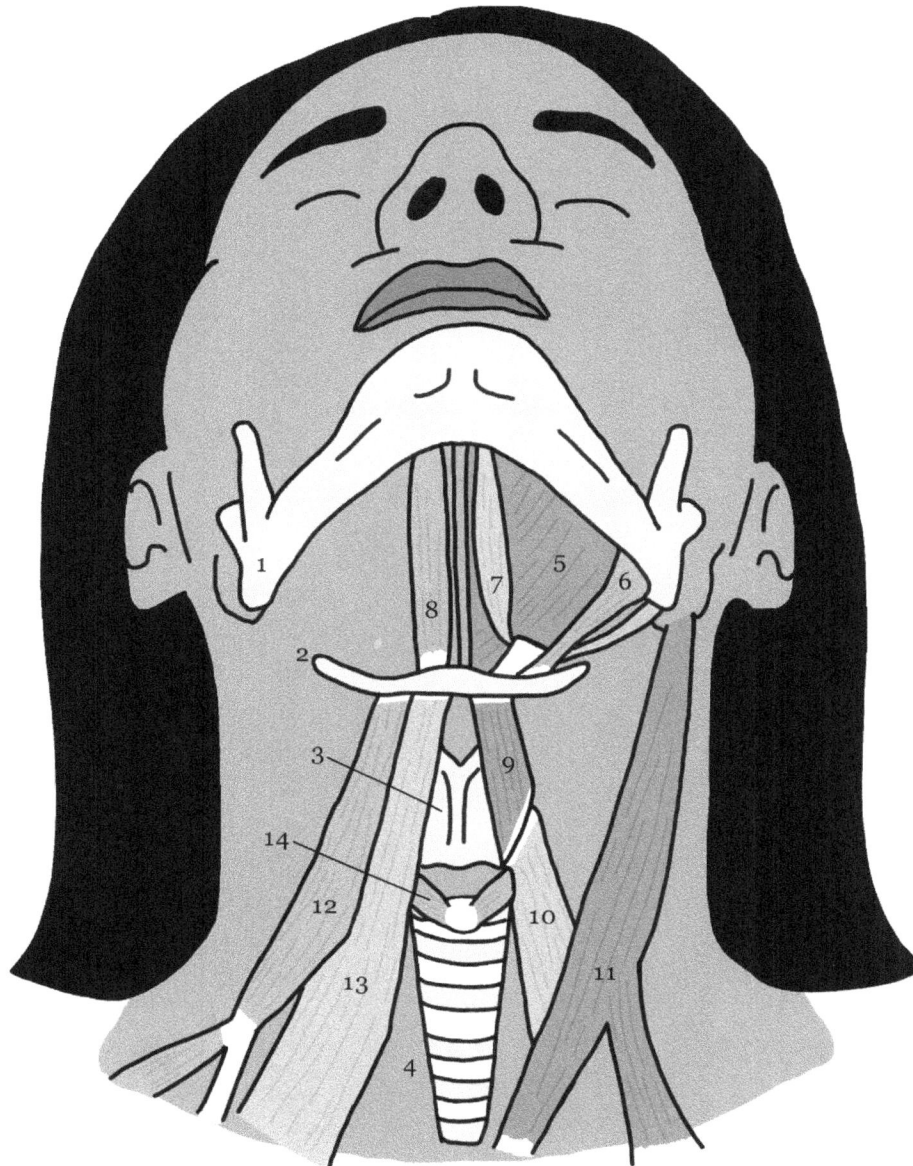

1. Mandible
2. Hyoid bone
3. Thyroid cartilage
4. Trachea
5. Mylohyoid

6. Stylohyoid
7. Digastric
8. Geniohyoid
9. Thyrohyoid
10. Sternothyroid

11. Sternocleidomastoid
12. Omohyoid
13. Sternohyoid
14. Cricothyroid

Dysarthria

Dysarthria

There are many strategies and exercises to treat dysarthria. The focus is usually on increasing intelligibility by treating the underlying speech subsystem (respiration, phonation, resonance, articulation, or prosody) that most affects your patient's ability to effectively and efficiently communicate. Use the principles of motor learning (Appendix) to help your patient learn and retain new movements.

Some patient may also benefit from medical intervention. Surgical options for dysarthria include procedures to the velopharynx, vocal folds, or diaphragm. Pharmacological options include medications for spasticity or tremors. Patients with velopharyngeal incompetence may benefit from surgery or a prosthesis to reduce hypernasal resonance. Work with their primary physician to refer out to a prosthodontist, dentist, plastic surgeon, etc., as appropriate. See the Resonance chapter for more details.

FYI, see the Appendix for a differential diagnosis chart to help you tell the difference between dysarthria, aphasia, and apraxia of speech.

Teamwork

Don't go it alone! If your patient needs support outside your scope of practice, bring in the team.

- Otolaryngologist if you suspect issues with the vocal folds or within the nasal, oral, laryngeal, or pharyngeal cavities
- Prosthodontist, dentist, or plastic surgeon to manage velopharyngeal incompetence
- Pharmacist to manage medications related to spasticity, tremors, etc.
- Physical therapist for positioning, functional mobility, LSVT BIG®
- Occupational therapist for help with cognitive treatment, fine motor treatment, ADLs, and IADLs
- Neurologist to diagnose and treat neurological impairments
- Audiologist to assess and manage hearing loss
- Medical social work for community resources
- Mental health professional to address mental health needs

Respiration

Symptoms of respiration issues include difficulties with inhalation/exhalation, difficulties controlling breathing for speech, reduced words per breath group, variable levels of loudness, and vocal fatigue. Many respiration treatment techniques target respiratory support and control.

You may treat respiration issues with:
- Intelligibility techniques
- Communication partner training
- Inspiratory checking
- Diaphragmatic breathing
- Breath control exercises
- Postural adjustments
- Add slash marks for breath groups to reading material. Depending on your patient, you'll add slashes every few syllables, words, or at phrase-level.
- Respiratory muscle strength training

Phonation

Difficulties with phonation can look like variable pitch, pitch breaks, abnormal vocal quality, audible inhalation or stridor, vocal tremors, monopitch, or diplophonia.

You may treat phonation issues with:
- Intelligibility techniques
- Communication partner training
- Breath control exercises (not recommended for patients with Parkinson's disease; Kalf et al., 2011; Newsome et al., 2017)
- Reviewing a speech breathing illustration
- LSVT, SPEAK OUT!, or Be Clear
- Hypoadduction treatment: head turn, manual therapy (lateralize thyroid), surgery referral
- Hyperadduction treatment: massage, relaxation
- Laryngeal exercises: cough for effortful closure, pull up on seat with hands, pitch glides, pitch matching
- See the Voice chapter for more information

Resonance

Difficulties with resonance can look like hypernasality or hyponasality.

You may treat resonance issues with:
- Biofeedback
- Over-articulation
- Refer for prostheses
- Labeling and negative practice
- See the Resonance chapter for more information

Articulation

Difficulties with articulation can look like slurred speech, imprecise consonants, and disfluencies.

You may treat articulation issues with:
- Communication partner education
- Clear speech strategies, including over-articulation
- Building up breath control
- Alphabet board or pacing board
- Hierarchy of speech sounds. The hierarchy, from the least to most challenging:
  - Sounds in isolation
  - Syllables
  - Words
  - Longer words
  - Minimal pairs
  - Phrases
  - Sentences
  - Paragraphs
  - Conversation
- Minimal contrasts
- Phonetic placement of the mouth, tongue, lips, jaw
- Multisyllabic words with consonant blends in varying positions
- Phone calls, conversations, interviews, monologues, phonemic lists
- Modeling, cueing, and providing video feedback

Prosody

Difficulties with prosody can manifest as a too-fast or too-slow speaking rate, excessive stress or lack of stress, rushes of speech, or a variable rate. Prosody treatment aims to make your patient's speech sound more natural and easier to understand.

You may treat prosody with:
- Intelligibility techniques
- Communication partner training
- Building up breath control
- Sentence stress, heteronyms
- Reduced speech rate
- Pacing (hand tapping, pacing board, metronome, delayed auditory feedback)
- Increasing loudness or overarticulation

Use visual cues to improve loudness, pitch, and duration. For example, you might use a gestures like placing a hand behind your ear to cue increased loudness or tilting your head as if you can't hear. Use any visual cue that makes sense to your patient (and doesn't annoy them!)

Add slash marks to longer reading tasks to cue when your patient should take a breath. Where the slash marks go will depend on your patient's current level of breath support. Try to match the breaths to natural pauses in speech, such as after a phrase or to emphasize an important point.

You can also teach your patient to vary their pitch or loudness if there is a communication breakdown. For example, if they see that a person doesn't understand, they repeat what they said louder or with a lower pitch.

Environmental Modifications

Improving the environment can help people with dysarthria stay safe and communicate more effectively (Brownlee, 2021; Cleveland Clinic, 2020; American Speech-Language-Hearing Association, n.d.a.)

Improve the environment
- Choose a quiet space. Turn off the TV and fans, shut doors (National Library of Medicine, 2022).
- Choose supportive seating.

Make communication easier
- Make sure everyone can see each other's faces. Turn on more lights, get closer, sit face-to-face.
- Have only one person speak at a time.
- Save important conversations for when they have more energy
- Stay hydrated. Sip water or use a humidifier if the air is dry
- Have AAC nearby, such as an alphabet board, pen and paper, or phone/tablet.
- Use a personal amplifier.
- Use video calls, like FaceTime or WhatsApp, instead of phone calls for the added visuals.
- Encourage everyone who needs it to wear their hearing aids and glasses.
- Use the free Telecommunication Relay Services, where an operator helps people with communication disorders make phone calls (National Relay Service in Australia, Relay U.K. in the United Kingdom).

Have emergency communication
- Have a quick way to call for a care partner inside the home, such as a wireless doorbell or call chime.
- Have a quick way to call for help outside of the home, such as text or personal emergency response system.
- Keep updated medical information on their phone or person.

Types of Dysarthria by Cause and Symptoms

Type	Possible Causes	Possible Symptoms
Flaccid	• Lower motor neuron damage • Trauma • Myasthenia gravis • Guillain-Barré syndrome	• Weakness • Breathiness • Short phrases • Hypernasality • Nasal emissions • Speaking on inhalation
Spastic	• Upper motor neuron damage • ALS • TBI • Multiple sclerosis • CVA	• Hypertonia • Slow rate • Strained vocal quality • Pitch breaks
Hypokinetic	• Basal ganglia damage • Parkinson's disease • TBI • CVA	• Rigidity • Reduced range of motion • Rushed speech • Monopitch, monoloudness • Flat affect • Tremor-like oral-motor movements
Ataxic	• Cerebellum damage • TBI • CVA • Degenerative diseases • Infections	• Reduced muscle coordination • Excess and equal stress • Distorted vowels • Lack of coordination in the jaw, face, and tongue

Hyperkinetic	• Basal ganglia damage • Huntington's disease • CVA	• Involuntary movements, motor tics, myoclonus • Distorted vowels • Intermittent vocal quality changes • Hypernasality • Excessive loudness variation
Unilateral Upper Motor Neuron	• Focal damage • Surgical trauma • Tumors • CVA	• Irregular articulatory breakdowns • Unilateral lower facial drooping • Unilateral lingual weakness • Hoarse vocal quality
Mixed	• TBI and CVA with multiple areas of the brain affected • ALS • Multiple sclerosis	• Slow speech • Prosody disrupted • Hypernasality • Strained voice • Various combinations of dysarthria types
Undetermined	• TBI • CVA • Neurogenic disorders	• Symptoms of dysarthria that don't fit into any of the other dysarthria types!

(American Speech-Language-Hearing Association, n.d.f.; Duffy, 2020)

Types of Dysarthria By Signs and Symptoms

	Flaccid	Spastic	Hypo.	Ataxic	Hyper.	UUMN
Weakness	✓	✓	✓	✓	✓	✓
Hypernasality	✓	-	-	-	✓	-
Short phrases	✓	-	-	-	-	-
Breathy	✓	-	-	-	✓	-
Fast speech rate	-	-	✓	-	-	-
Slow speech rate	-	✓	-	-	✓	✓
Strained voice	-	✓	-	-	✓	✓
Distorted vowel	-	-	-	✓	✓	-
Tremors	-	-	✓	✓	✓	-
Rigidity	-	-	✓	-	-	-
Motor tics	-	-	-	-	✓	-
Irregular articulatory breakdowns	-	-	-	✓	-	✓

Breath Control

Use this breath control technique to help your patient take deep enough breaths to speak more clearly.

Breath control protocol:

1. Ask your patient to breathe in slowly for 3 seconds.

2. Hold for 3 seconds.

3. Release their breath out slowly for 3 seconds.

4. Continue for a few more rounds.

5. Say each sound for as long as they can:
    ○ hhh
    ○ sss
    ○ thhh
    ○ fff
    ○ Shhh

6. Say each sound for as long as they can:
    ○ hhha, hhhoe, hhhi, hhhow, whhho,
    ○ sssah, ssso, sssee, sssow, sssue
    ○ ttthaw, thhho, thhhee, thhhow, thhhew
    ○ fffa, fffoe, fffee, fffow, fffoo
    ○ shhha, shhhow, shhhe, shhhaow, shhhoe

Lee Silverman Voice Treatment

LSVT _OUD (LSVT LOUD) is an evidence-based voice treatment program for patients with Parkinson's disease and other neurological conditions. Its goal and focus are to improve vocal loudness. It teaches patients to think loud, work hard, and recalibrate what their "normal" voice is.

LSVT LOUD has an intensive schedule of 16 1-hour treatment sessions (4 sessions per week for 4 weeks), plus daily homework. LSVT-X is an option for patients who can only do 2 sessions per week.

LSVT was developed by Lorraine Ramig. You can get trained and certified on the LSVT LOUD website.

Main components of LSVT LOUD treatment:

1. Your patient sustains "ah" using a loud voice for as long as they can. Repeat a set number of times:
   - First, in their habitual pitch.
   - Then, at their highest comfortable pitch.
   - Finally, at their lowest comfortable pitch.

2. They read a list of functional phrases over and over using a loud voice.

3. They complete other drills, such as reading paragraphs aloud or having a conversation using a loud voice.

4. They complete daily homework, which include drills from in-session practice and a carryover assignment (e.g. ordering coffee at their favorite cafe while thinking loud).

SPEAK OUT!

SPEAK OUT! is a voice treatment program developed by the Parkinson's Voice Project. It aims to help people with Parkinson's disease produce a stronger, clearer voice by learning to "speak with intent." Treatment consists of 8-12 speech therapy sessions that run 3 times per week for 4 weeks, plus daily homework.

The program offers many supports, including weekly groups and extensive follow-up. You can learn how to do this treatment on the SPEAKOUT! website (Parkinson Voice Project, n.d.)

Main SPEAK OUT! treatment components (Sullivan et al., 2024; Watts, 2016; Reid Health, n.d.):
- Vocal warm-up
- Vowel prolongation
- Gliding and intonation exercises
- Automatic sequences, such as counting
- Reading aloud sentences to paragraphs of gradually increasing length and complexity
- Cognitive tasks, such as discussing needed items for different scenarios

Be Clear

Be Clear aims to improve speech intelligibility in people with dysarthria caused by a traumatic brain injury or stroke. It's based on clear speech and the principles of motor learning and neuroplasticity. Be Clear may improve speech rate and intelligibility (Park et al., 2016; Whelan et al., 2022). The program has an intensive treatment schedule of 4 1-hour sessions per week for 4 weeks, plus 15 minutes of daily homework.

Example Be Clear treatment session protocol (Park et al., 2016): Throughout treatment, the patient will focus on speaking using clear speech.

1. **Pre-practice**
   - Model/show a video of someone reading a passage with normal speech and then reading the same passage with clear speech. Your patient identifies which is easier to understand and why.
   - Your patient reads the same passage using clear speech. Provide specific feedback as needed ("use big speech movements" or "slow down").

2. **Treatment**
   - Practice 10 functional phrases. For example, "Did you feed the cat?" 5 times each.
   - Practice 10 service request phrases. For example, "Where is the restroom?" 5 times each.
   - Practice functional speech tasks: Complete 3 speech tasks that are functional and meaningful to your patient. For example, reading, picture description, or conversation. Spend 10 minutes on each speech task.
   - Give feedback about results (e.g., "that was clear" or "that was unclear").

3. **Do homework**
   - Your patient practices the functional phrases, service requests, and functional speech tasks at home for 15 minutes daily.
   - Assign "transfer" tasks (make a phone call, order a drink) to help with generalization (Park et al., 2016).

Biofeedback

Use biofeedback to help patients with dysarthria have greater awareness of their dysarthria symptoms (reduced loudness, fast speech rate, etc.)

Mirror under the nose
Use this with patients who have mild hypernasality. Place a small mirror (e.g., dental mirror, cosmetics mirror) under your patient's nose. Ask them to say a sentence with NO nasal sounds ("see you later" or "please take the plate"). The mirror should not fog up if their resonance is normal. If it does fog up and hypernasality is impacting their ability to communicate their wants and needs, consider treatment and/or referral to an ENT.

Voice recorder
After getting appropriate permissions, record your patient talking using a voice recorder (e.g. a voice recording app).

Ask your patient to listen to their own voice and analyze their loudness, speech rate, intelligibility, etc. Hearing themselves can increase self-awareness. For example, hearing themselves on a recording may help a patient with Parkinson's disease realize that their voice is quiet compared to others in the recording.

You can also record a patient using their strategies then not using the strategies—and compare the difference. This may increase buy-in that the strategies are working!

Delayed auditory feedback (DAF)
Use DAF with patients who speak so fast that they have reduced intelligibility or comprehensibility. DAF allows patients to hear themselves speak with a slight delay, which can help them talk more slowly. Although DAF devices can be pricey, affordable DAF apps are now available to download.

Apraxia

Apraxia

Apraxia of speech (AOS) treatment involves a lot of intensive drills. This is so that patients can relearn motor sequences. According to the principles of motor learning, practicing challenging targets improves generalization, but tasks shouldn't be so hard that your patient can't accurately produce the target. Choose the right level of challenge to increase motivation and decrease frustration. See how to modify treatment difficulty below.

You'll often begin at the syllable level and then progress to monosyllabic words, multisyllabic words, phrases, sentences, paragraphs, and then conversation. For severe apraxia, you may need to start at the phoneme level. Use the principles of motor learning (Appendix) with any apraxia treatment task to help your patient learn and retain new movements

In general, to make a task easier, incorporate:
- Shorter syllables
- Automatic speech
- Repeating a model
- Comparing oral versus nasal sounds
- Bilabials, linguals, and alveolar sounds
- Consonant clusters between syllables
- Stressed syllables
- High-frequency syllables

To make a task harder, incorporate:
- Longer syllables
- Volitional speech
- Self-generated utterances
- Comparing voiced versus voiceless sounds
- Consonant clusters within syllables
- Unstressed syllables and words
- Low-frequency syllables and words

See the Appendix for a differential diagnosis chart to help you tell the difference between apraxia of speech, dysarthria, and, aphasia.

Teamwork

Don't go it alone! Bring in the team if your patient needs support outside your scope of practice.

- Neurology to diagnose and treat underlying neurological impairments
- Occupational and physical therapy for limb apraxia management
- Support groups for people with strokes, brain injuries, etc.
- Pharmacy to manage medications related to spasticity, tremors, etc.
- Audiologist to assess and manage hearing loss
- Medical social work for community resources
- Mental health professional to address mental health needs

Integral Stimulation

Integral stimulation uses sensory cues (visual, auditory, tactile, etc.) to help patients produce the target sound. Treatment approaches such as Sound Production Treatment incorporate integral stimulation into their protocols.

If your patient has multiple target sounds, start with targets that are easier for them. Refer to the cueing hierarchy below for guidance on how to support your patients using sensory cues (Rosenbek et al., 1973; Philippine Academy of Rehabilitation Medicine, 2017; Duffy, 2020).

Cueing hierarchy for Integral Stimulation:

Clinician	Patient	Sensory Cue
1. Model. "Listen to me, watch me, do what I do."	Your patient first listens and watches, then repeats the word in unison with the clinician.	Auditory, Visual
2. Model then mouth. First, model the target. Then, mouth the target as your patient repeats it aloud.	They listen and watch. Then, they repeat the target as the clinician mouths it.	Fading Auditory, Visual
3. Model then pause. Pause as they repeat back without assistance.	They listen and watch the model. Then, they repeat back without assistance.	Fading Visual, Fading Auditory
4. Model then pause longer. Ask them to repeat back the target 3 times without assistance.	They listen and watch the model. Then they repeat back 3 times without assistance.	Fading Visual, Fading Auditory
5. Write. Show the written target (and/or image) without saying or mouthing the target. Ask them to say the target.	They view the written target/image. Then, they say the target aloud without further assistance.	Written, No Visual, No Auditory
6. Write then remove. Present the written target, remove it, and then ask them to say the target.	They view the written target, and then say the word after it is removed.	Fading Written, No Visual, No Auditory
7. Question. Prompt the target by asking a question.	They answer the question by saying the target word without assistance.	No sensory cueing
8. Role play. Role-play a situation to elicit the target.	They say the word in response to the situation without assistance.	No sensory cueing

(Rosenbek et al., 1973)

Sound Production Treatment (SPT)

SPT, developed by Julie Wambaugh and colleagues, uses Integral Stimulation and the principles of motor learning to treat specific sound errors. Evidence shows that it improves the production of trained sounds in people with apraxia of speech, including severe AOS, chronic AOS, and verbal perseverations. SPT may be appropriate for patients who can follow simple commands and repeat single-syllable words.

Preparation
- Choose 2-3 target sounds that focus on your patient's sound errors.
- For monosyllabic target words, you may need to use a minimal pair. The minimal pair may change as your patient improves.

Sound Production Treatment protocol:

1. Model the target word. Ask for repetition.
   - After any response, give feedback.
   - **Correct.** If your patient is correct at any point: Ask for 5 repetitions. Then move on to the next target word.
   - **Incorrect.** If incorrect, choose a word that sounds like what they just said (the minimal pair). Model the minimal pair.
   - **Still incorrect.** If still incorrect, say, 'Watch me, listen to me, say it with me." Then say the minimal pair with your patient up to 3 times.
   - **Still incorrect.** If still incorrect, go to step 2.

2. Write down the target sound, model the target word, and then ask for repetition.
   - After any response, give feedback.
   - **Correct.** If your patient is correct at any point: Ask for 5 repetitions. Then, move on to the next target word.
   - **Incorrect.** If incorrect, go to step 3.

3. Say, "Watch me, listen to me, and say it with me." Then, say the target word with your patient up to 3 times.
   - After any response, give feedback.
   - **Correct.** If your patient is correct at any point: Ask for 5 repetitions. Then, move on to the next target word.
   - **Incorrect.** If incorrect, go to step 4.

4. Give error-specific articulatory placement cues for the target word. Say, "Watch me, listen to me, and say it with me," then say the target word with your patient.
    ○ After any response, give feedback.
    ○ **Correct.** If your patient is correct at any point: Ask for 5 repetitions. Then, move on to the next target word.
    ○ **Incorrect.** If incorrect, start over at step 1 with a new word.

(Mauszycki & Wambaugh, 2020; Wambaugh & Mauszycki, 2010; Wambaugh et al., 1998; Wambaugh et al., 2021; Wambaugh, n.d.)

Multiple Input Phoneme Therapy (MIPT)

MIPT is typically used with patients who have severe AOS and aphasia. MIPT helps patients gain control of their stereotypic utterances and then build on them to say a wider variety of words. For example, if your patient's stereotypic utterance is "hello," MIPT can help shape it into other /h/ initial monosyllabic words.

Multiple Input Phoneme Therapy protocol:

1. Write down your patient's stereotypic utterance(s). This utterance will be the starting point for treatment.
   - e.g. The stereotypic utterance is "hello."
2. Model the stereotypic utterance while giving a gestural/prosodic cue.
   - Model "hello," while tapping their arm.
   - They repeat "hello," as you tap their arm.
3. Repeat 6-10 times.
   - The goal of these steps is for you to gain control of their stereotypic utterance. This means that they only say it when you cue it.
4. Fade the cues until you're silently modeling the word while miming the gesture. Your patient says the stereotypic utterance as you mime the gesture.
   - They say "hello," as you mime tapping their arm.
5. Choose a new target word that has the same initial phoneme as the stereotypic utterance.
   - e.g. New target word is "help."
6. Repeat steps 2 and 3 with the new target. Do this 5-10 times.
   - Model, "help" while tapping their arm.
   - Mouth the word, then mime tapping only as they say, "help."
7. Increase the challenge of the target words.
   - Build up to consonant blends, multisyllabic words, sentences, etc.

(Stevens & Glaser, 1983; American Speech-Language-Hearing Association, n.d.c.)

Melodic Intonation Therapy (MIT)

MIT is an evidence-based treatment for patients who have apraxia and/or non-fluent aphasia secondary to a stroke (Sparks et al., 1974; Sparks & Holland, 1976; Zumbansen et al., 2014).

Melodic Intonation Therapy protocol:

1. Show your patient the target phrase.
2. Hum at a rate of 1 syllable per second.
   - Use a higher-pitched note on the stressed syllable or word.
3. Sing and tap the phrase twice: While singing, you tap your patient's left hand on each syllable.
   - Again, sing a higher-pitched note on the stressed syllable or word.
   - For example, with the word "apple," the first syllable "ah" will be higher-pitched, and the second syllable "ple" will be lower-pitched.
4. Sing the phrase in unison with your patient while tapping their left hand on each syllable.
5. Continue to sing the phrase together while tapping their left hand. Gradually fade your singing.
   - Now, your patient is singing alone while you tap their left hand (don't give verbal or oral/facial cueing).
6. Take turns singing: You sing the phrase while your patient listens. Stop singing so that they sing the phrase alone, but keep tapping their left hand.
7. Patient sings alone: Immediately after a correct production, ask, "What did you say?" Tap their hand as they sing the target phrase.
8. Repeat a new phrase.

Gradually make it more challenging by increasing delays between model and response, changing the melody to sound more natural, and increasing the length between model and response.

(Norton et al., 2009; Zumbansen et al., 2014; Zumbansen & Tremblay, 2019; Helm-Estabrooks, 1989)

Script Training

Script training helps patients gain small 'islands' of relatively fluent, automatic speech by practicing a script (Youmans et al., 2011). Help your patients identify what scripts would be helpful to their lives, such as ordering at a favorite restaurant, refilling a prescription, or greeting a neighbor. Help them create the script and then practice it over and over again.

Creating scripts:

- Choose a script topic that's relevant to your patient.
- Match the script level with your patient's apraxia severity.
- Add in personalized content: for example, add in the name of their town or the name of a loved one.
- Increase the difficulty of the scripts as your patient's intelligibility improves.
    - Increase the readability difficulty: increase the number of syllables, words, and then sentences in the script.
    - Increase the syntactic difficulty: use complex vs. simple sentences.
    - Increase the semantic difficulty: use more complex, less frequent, or longer words.

(Kaye & Cherney, 2016)

Pacing Techniques

Pacing techniques can improve communication in people with apraxia of speech by slowing down speech rate and improving prosody.

Pacing boards

Pacing boards are an effective way to reduce speech rate and increase intelligibility. They often come as plastic trays with raised ridges. Your patient slides their finger across the ridge as they say each syllable (Wambaugh, n.d.) Once your patient gets the hang of speaking using a pacing board, they can pace by tapping on their thigh. This makes pacing less obvious and more functional in daily life.

Metronome

Set the metronome to a rate slightly slower than your patient's habitual speech rate. Have them read aloud at one syllable or word per beat. For added feedback, they can tap along to the beat. Use a cueing hierarchy as needed.

Hand tapping

Similar to using a metronome, tap the table at a rate slightly slower than your patient's habitual speech rate. Have them read aloud at one syllable or word per beat. Use a cueing hierarchy as needed.

Example pacing technique protocol:

1. Model it, then do it together.
   - For example, you each have a pacing board. You model reading aloud while sliding your finger across the board one syllable at a time. Then, your patient does it in unison with you.
2. Model it, then they copy.
   - For example, you model speaking with the pacing board. Then, your patient copies you as you watch and listen.
3. Gradually fade cues as they continue.
   - For example, read the first few words using the pacing board in unison with your patient. Gradually fade your reading and pointing so that they are reading alone.
4. Work up to more challenging targets. Model and cue as needed. Increase the challenge by increasing the reading rate to a more normal rate, pacing per word versus per syllable, reading longer material, etc.
5. Gradually work up to using the pacing technique independently.

Environmental Modifications

Simple environmental changes can make communication easier and more effective for people with apraxia of speech. Here are some ideas:

Improve the environment
- Choose a quiet space with less background noise (Steffy et al., 2017).
- If needed, move somewhere quieter with better acoustics and lighting.

Make communication easier
- Make sure everyone can see each other's faces: turn on more lights, get closer, sit face-to-face.
- Encourage only one person to speak at a time.
- Use AAC, such as an alphabet board, texting, or writing.
- Encourage everyone who needs it to wear their hearing aids and glasses.
- Use the free Telecommunication Relay Services, where an operator helps people with communication disorders make phone calls (National Relay Service in Australia, Relay U.K. in the United Kingdom).

Have emergency communication
- Have a quick way to call for help inside the home, such as a wireless doorbell or call chime.
- Have a quick way to call for help outside of the home, such as text or a personal emergency response system.
- Keep updated medical information on their phone or person.

Memory

Memory

Speech therapy memory treatment can be divided into **internal options** (e.g. memory strategies) and **external options** (e.g. visual aids). Patients often benefit from using both.

Errorless learning improves learning in people with memory impairments (Ehlhardt et al., 2008). To do errorless learning, focus on accuracy when teaching a new skill. Discourage guessing, model the correct answer, and give plenty of cues. Also use **fading cues**. Start by giving plenty of cues to help your patient experience success. Gradually decrease (fade) the amount of cueing as they get the hang of the task.

Teamwork

Don't go it alone! Bring in the team if your patient needs support outside your scope of practice:

- Occupational therapy for help with cognitive treatment, fine motor treatment, ADLs, and IADLs
- Physical therapy for help with positioning and functional mobility
- Neurology to diagnose and treat neurological impairments
- Audiologist to assess and manage hearing loss
- Medical social work for community resources
- Support groups for people with strokes, brain injuries, dementia, etc.
- Mental health professional to address mental health needs

Memory Strategies

Memory strategies can be a good starting point for patients with moderate or severe memory impairments.

Pay Attention
Before or during a task, your patient may need prompts to attend to the target information. Ask your patient to "Listen, look, and focus on what you want to remember."

Take a Mental Picture
Ask your patient to "Visualize what you want to remember and store it in your brain." This can be helpful when they want to remember the location of an item, such as where they set their keys.

Repeat and Rehearse
This is the go-to memory strategy for many people because it's easy to use and is often already familiar to them. Ask your patient to "Repeat what you just learned over and over." They can repeat the name of the person they just met, the date of a newly made appointment, or the next step of a recipe they're following.

Write it Down
Ask your patient to "Write down what you want to remember." This is another go-to memory strategy that can be used with any severity of memory impairment. Pair it with other strategies, including "repeat and rehearse" and "use external reminders."

Use External Reminders
Encourage your patient to use whatever is readily available or familiar to them, such as a watch, calendar, planner, notepad, Notes app on their smartphone, smart speaker, or sticky note. You can also pair other strategies like "repeat and rehearse" and "take a mental picture" to help them remember what is written.

Chunk and Organize Information
Ask your patient to "Sort lists of information into categories." Use this when your patient has a lot of information to remember, such as a list of groceries. They can sort the list by type (dairy, frozen, fruits, etc.) or location in the store.

Make Associations

Ask your patients with milder memory deficits to "Make connections between what you want to remember and what you already know." For example, they can connect the name of someone they just met to someone with the same name.

Functional Memory Treatment

Functional tasks are the activities that patients want and need to do in their daily lives. They're meaningful, motivating, and can improve safety, independence, and quality of life.

How to know what's functional. Interview your patient and their caregiver. Their answers will help you know what's functional for your patient. Ask about:
- Your patient's previous level of functioning (PLOF) schedule
- Their schedule now
- The difference between their current and PLOF schedules
- How much help they receive now vs. PLOF
- Their goals
- Their likes, dislikes, hobbies, preferences, needs and wants

How to make memory treatment functional. Do tasks that:
- They were previously able to do but can't/don't do now
- Help them reach their goals
- Are based on their likes and hobbies
- Are based on their needs and wants
- Incorporate materials from your patient's life and daily surroundings

How to make worksheets as functional as possible.
- Pair memory worksheets with strategies that your patient is stimulable for, then help your patient identify ways to use these strategies in daily life.
  - For example, practice the "associations" strategy with a worksheet. Then, ask your patient to use the strategy to remember an appointment.

For patients with progressive conditions.
The goal is to maintain function for as long as possible.
- Educate caregivers on how to support your patient.
- If they have mild cognitive impairment, introduce ways to avoid memory loss (healthy diet, exercise, good quality sleep, socialize, etc.)
- Refer to neurology if they're not yet diagnosed with a progressive condition, but you see the signs of one.

Functional memory treatment ideas.

Orient to self, time, place, and other people
- Mild or moderate memory impairment: remember specific names or things, like their therapy team's names.
- Severe memory impairment: use a calendar, memory book, and other visual aids to decrease confusion/anxiety and increase orientation.

Safety & Health
- Mild memory impairment: safety tasks related to independent money and medication management and other IADLs.
- Moderate memory impairment: safety tasks related to increasing independence with ADLs and IADLs.
- Severe memory impairment: basic safety tasks related to remembering precautions, asking for help, avoiding falls, etc.

Schedules
- Mild memory impairment: tasks for independent time management (keeping track of appointments using a smartphone or planner).
- Moderate memory impairment: tasks to increase independence in time management (checking calendars, setting alarms).
- Severe memory impairment: tasks to decrease confusion/anxiety, like visual schedules and posted signs.

Medication Management
- Mild memory impairment: tasks for independent medication management, like sorting medications and refilling prescriptions.
- Moderate memory impairment: tasks that increase awareness of medications by reviewing the medication list.

Lifestyle Changes to Support Memory

Discuss ways to improve memory and reduce the risk of memory loss with your patients, especially those with mild cognitive impairment or who are at risk for memory loss.

Improve overall physical health. Encourage your patient to:
- Eat a healthy diet and maintain a healthy weight.
- Do physical exercise. Aerobic exercise and resistance training may improve memory. Your patient should talk with their doctor about the best exercise plan for them.
- Quit smoking.
- Check their hearing and wear hearing aids if they need it.
- Get 7-9 hours of high-quality sleep every night.
- Talk with their doctor about managing hypertension, diabetes, depression, anxiety, and other issues that increase the risk of developing dementia.

Engage the brain
- Encourage your patient to engage in mental exercise, including reading, learning something new, or memorizing short lists.

Socialize
- Encourage your patient to meet with friends or family, join a club or group, visit community centers, volunteer, etc.

(Broadhouse et al., 2020; Livingston et al., 2020; Nicola et al., 2024; Petersen et al., 2018; Reiner, 2020; Saban et al., 2022)

Spaced Retrieval

Spaced retrieval helps people with memory loss remember new information (Benigas, n.d.b.; Hopper et al., 2005; Oren et al., 2014). Use it for safety, orientation, answering repetitive questions, etc.

How to use spaced retrieval based on severity
First trial spaced retrieval with your patient to see if it works for them. For patients with severe memory impairment, you can use spaced retrieval to recall specific information related to safety, orientation, or repetitive questions. For moderate impairments, use spaced retrieval to recall specific important information, such as an upcoming appointment.

Spaced retrieval protocol:

1. **Ask the question.** It should be specific and open-ended (can't be answered with "yes"/"no"). Keep it short, using their own words.
   - "When is your eye appointment?"

2. **Give the correct response.** This is the exact response you will expect in the next step.
   - "Tuesday at 10 am"

3. **Ask the exact same question again, and wait for a response.** The answer should be the exact correct response you taught ("Tuesday at 10 am").
   - If incorrect, go back to step 1.
   - If correct, wait 15 seconds and ask the same question again.

4. **Wait, then ask again.** Continue to increase the time between asking the question.
   - Start with 15 seconds, increasing to 30 seconds, 60 seconds, 2 minutes, 4 minutes, 8 minutes, etc. You may go up to a half-hour and beyond.

If incorrect at any step, go back to step 1.

TEACH-M

TEACH-M is an acronym for a systematic method of teaching cognitive skills to patients after a traumatic brain injury or related condition. It was initially designed to teach multi-step skills to patients with severe memory and executive functioning deficits, post-TBI (Cicerone et al., 2022; Ehlhardt et al., 2008).

Task analysis helps patients learn new skills by breaking down a task into smaller steps. Teach each smaller step, then 'chain' them together.

Errorless learning. The goal is for your patient to make as few errors as possible as they learn a new skill or step of a skill.

First, model the skill. Focus on accuracy, emphasize not guessing, and cue as needed. If an error happens, give enough cues to get the correct response. For example, model the skill again.

Assessment. Monitor patient progress. This is something you already do to document daily notes and reports. For milder impairments, teach patients to assess and monitor their own performance.

Cumulative review. Your patient reviews all of the steps they've learned at least once before attempting the task.

High number of practice trials. Your patient completes the entire task over and over again. Prioritize doing the task correctly (errorless learning) over the number of repetitions.

Metacognition. Patients need to be aware of their cognitive deficits for treatment to be the most effective.
- Before the task, ask your patient to predict how they'll do.
- After the task, ask them to assess how they did.
- After the task, discuss how their prediction compares to how they actually did.

Meaningful. We added an extra M! Meaningful treatment leads to better results.

Dementia Treatment

Memory treatment for dementia often focuses on external memory aids such as reminder cards and memory books to improve orientation, reduce confusion and agitation, and increase quality of life. Treatment also emphasizes training family and care partner in the use of external memory aids and in techniques such as spaced retrieval.

Beyond compensatory strategies and care partner training, dementia treatment may also include approaches such as Cognitive Stimulation Therapy and Montessori for Dementia.

Cognitive Stimulation Therapy

Cognitive Stimulation Therapy (CST) is a group treatment program for people with mild to moderate dementia. It was developed by Aimee Spector and colleagues (Aguirre et al., 2013).

CST uses activities to stimulate cognitive skills in a way that targets people with dementia's cognitive weaknesses (memory, language, executive functioning) while drawing on their remaining strengths (reminiscing, reading, social enjoyment, and routines). The activities are designed to be fun and engaging, ranging from discussions, to trivia, to cooking.

You can buy the small group manual, instructor's manual, and/or one-on-one treatment manual from the University College London.

Montessori for Dementia

Montessori is a philosophical approach to aging and dementia. The Montessori approach focusing on designing the environment to nurture the needs, interests, and abilities of the person with dementia (Brush & Bourgeois, 2020).
- Materials are neatly organized, labeled, and easy to access
- There are hands-on, individual-led activities available at all times
- Activities are joyful, engaging, and satisfying
- Emphasize maximizing choice, freedom of movement, and independence
- Use lots of visual aids

External Memory Aids

External memory aids are an evidence-based treatment option for mild to severe memory disorders (Jones et al., 2021; Scullin et al., 2022; Sohlberg et al., 2007). Use whatever external aids is readily available, familiar, and that your patient is willing and able to use.

Example external memory aids by severity:
- Mild memory impairment: smartphone, planner, calendar, checklists
- Moderate: weekly or monthly calendar, sticky notes
- Severe: visual schedule, memory books/wallets, reminder cards

Memory books & wallets

A memory book or wallet can help a patient orient to where they are and what's happening around them. This can decrease anxiety and repetitive questions (Bourgeois, 2015; May & Murray, 2019). It can also unearth emotions that trigger memories. Use memory books or wallets with patients who have severe memory impairments or dementia. Give plenty of care partner training and support. Download a free Memory Book template at adultspeechtherapy.co (search "memory book").

Reminder cards

Reminder cards are written information that remind a patient of something important. They're often posted strategically around their environment. As always, the reminder cards are best if they are functional, meaningful, and formatted for your patient. Reminder cards can come in many forms. Below are just a few examples of how to use them to support your patient's goals:
- Room number with name posted next to their door
- Wheelchair safety attached to wheelchair
- Answer to a repetitive question on a lanyard
- Bathroom sign
- Personal identification card kept in wallet
- Daily schedule on the refrigerator
- Swallowing strategy framed on the dining table
- Labels in the closet
- Discussion cards during group discussions
- Modified recipe card for when a grandchild visits

Environmental Modifications

Modifying the environment can help people with memory deficits improve their safety, independence, and quality of life.

Reduce distractions
- Reduce background noise: Close doors and windows, turn off the TV
- Reduce visual distractions: Get rid of clutter such as extra furniture, extra wall art, papers, and mirrors
- Try not to talk during important tasks

Improve the space
- Improve lighting: add lamps, reduce glare, avoid flickering or fluorescent lights
- Add visual contrast: use high-contrast colors to highlight an obstacle or important item (e.g. place white reflective tape on a dark step)
- Improve acoustics: close curtains, use noise-canceling headphones
- Arrange furniture to create open walkways and make a clear line of sight to important things, such as the bathroom or clock

Organize
- Assign specific places for specific things: keys on a hook by the door
- Use bins and shelves
- Add labels: drawers, pantry, toiletries
- Add signs: next to the restroom or dining room

Give information
- Post their schedule on a calendar or memo board
- Put up a large digital clock
- Set alarms for tasks/events such as taking their medications
- Post step-by-step cards for tasks, like how to lock their wheelchair
- Use memory aids, such as a memory book or wallet

(American Speech-Language-Hearing Association, n.d.e., Brush et al., 2012; Hickey, n.d.)

When to modify the environment, by severity
- Mild memory impairment: Use any during complex tasks (multi-step, challenging, etc.)
- Moderate: Use any when doing moderate to complex tasks
- Severe: Use any or all when doing any cognitive task

Attention

Attention

Attention treatment aims to help patients better attend throughout their day to improve their safety, independence, and quality of life. For each task you present, know whether you're targeting sustained, selective, alternating, or divided attention/working memory. This will help you focus on the goal behavior and make data collection easier.

In general, follow the **hierarchy of attention.** Focused attention is at the bottom of the hierarchy of attention (Sohlberg & Mateer, 2001; Cicerone et al., 2022). Above focused attention is sustained, selective, alternating, and then divided attention (or working memory). Start treatment at the sustained attention level or wherever your patient needs support. Once they master this foundational ability, they will move up the hierarchy to the next level of attention.

To measure attention, use one of these methods:
- Time how many seconds they sustain attention before needing a cue or repetition.
- Count how many cues they need within a specific time frame to sustain attention.
- Count how many cues they need during a specific task to sustain attention.

Also use **task analysis** (Powell et al., 2012). Help your patient break down a task into smaller steps. Teach them each smaller step, then 'chain' them together.

Target metacognition to help patients improve awareness about how they did on a task. Metacognition is key to improved attention. Before the task, ask your patient to predict how they'll do. After the task, ask them to assess how they did. Discuss how their prediction compares with how they actually did. Then, make a plan for what strategies and supports may help support their attention next time.

Finally, **use repetition.** Patients need a high level of repetition so that what they learn in treatment becomes an automatic behavior. Follow the principles of neuroplasticity.

Teamwork

Don t go it alone! Bring in the team if your patient needs support outside your scope of practice.

- Occupational therapy for help with cognitive treatment, fine motor treatment, ADLs, and IADLs
- Physical therapy for help with positioning and functional mobility
- Neurology to diagnose and treat neurological impairments
- Audiology to assess and manage hearing loss
- Medical social work for community resources
- Support groups for people with strokes or other brain injuries

Attention Strategies

Trial a strategy to see if it clicks with your patient. If it helps your patient get back on track with minimal frustration, stick with it. If not, try a different strategy.

Gradually work towards building a repertoire of strategies.
The goal is for your patient to independently use the strategy in their daily life.

P.A.S.E.
An acronym for Pause, Ask, Steps, Execute. Teach your patient to identify when they have stopped paying attention. Then, teach them to walk through each step of P.A.S.E. to get back on track.

- Pause. Your patient pauses their mind and body. They take a slow, deep breath.
- Ask. They take a mental step back to ask themselves: "What do want to be doing? What's my goal?"
- Steps. They make a plan. They list the steps to accomplishing their goal.
- Execute. They follow their plan to complete the goal task.

Pause, Breathe, Return
- Pause. Your patient pauses their body and mind to identify when they're not paying attention or are feeling overwhelmed.
- Breathe. They take 3 slow, deep breaths to calm and recenter.
- Return. They bring this calm back to the task they're doing.

The 3 W's
When they get off task, these are three questions your patient can ask themselves:
- What am I doing?
- What was I doing before?
- What should I do next?

Pace Yourself (Weightman et al., 2014)

Encourage your patient to take breaks. This can be after a set amount of time or after they complete a specific task. During the break, have them check in with their fatigue and attention levels. If they seem good, they continue with their day. If not, they should take a longer break or add attention strategies and modifications.

Write it Down

Train patients to take notes, especially if they're in the middle of a task. Designate a tool, like a notepad or a smartphone app, to always have on hand to jot down notes. This can help patients save off-task thoughts for later. Set a timer or an alarm for when to return to these notes.

Self-Talk (Cicerone et al., 2022).

Train patients to talk themselves through a task. This can prevent distractions and reduce errors. When first learning a task, they say each step aloud to themselves. As they improve at the task, they whisper the steps to themselves. Finally, they use "inner speech" and talk through the steps in their head.

They can also ask themselves questions to stay on track. "What am I doing? What do I need to focus on? What else do I need to do?"

Levels of self-talk:
- Self-talk with a visual aid, such as written instructions of what to do
- Self-talk: talking to oneself while completing the task to stay on track
- Whispered self-talk
- Inner self-talk, the ultimate goal. Your patient silently talks through the steps in their head

Environmental Modifications

Modify your patient's environment to make it easier to pay attention. Improving the environment can help improve their attention, safety, and independence (American Speech-Language-Hearing Association, n.c.b; Cicerone et al., 2022; Weightman et al., 2015).

Remove distractions
- Reduce background noise and visual distractions.
- Reduce clutter: Remove papers and extra decor, have clutter-free zones for workspaces.
- Use a 'Do Not Disturb' sign when and where they need to focus.
- Turn off the TV, turn off cell phone notifications, close doors and windows, ask others to leave.
- Move to a quieter space or use noise-cancelling headphones.

Get organized
- Assign specific places for specific things (keys go on a hook by the door).
- Place loose items into labeled bins.
- Set reminders and alarms.
- Post a schedule on a calendar or memo board.
- Make lists and plans, such as a to-do list, grocery list, etc.
- Have a filing system for important documents.
- Set up systems to pay bills, refill medications, etc.

Improve daily routines
- Have a routine, such as for morning, bedtime and work.
- Do one thing at a time. Don't multitask. When in a conversation, everyone should take turns talking.
- Choose the best time of day to do important tasks, such as when they're less tired or when a care partner can help.
- Take breaks.

Functional Attention Treatment

Tasks such as card sorting and cancellation have their place and can be a great way to initially teach attention strategies, but it's best to transition to functional tasks as soon they are able. Functional tasks are activities that patients want and need to do in their daily lives. They're meaningful and motivating and can improve safety, independence, and quality of life.

Here are tips for keeping your attention treatment as functional as possible so that they generalize into patients' daily lives.

Connect attention tasks to their ADLs and IADLs
Gather information about your patient's:
- Previous level of functioning, including how much help they needed with ADLs and IADLs
- Typical schedule before their injury
- Current level of functioning. Including how much help they now need with ADLs and IADLs
- Current schedule

Compare their former and current abilities, need for help, and schedule. Work towards closing this gap during attention treatment.

Do language-based tasks
Many language-based tasks, such as reading, writing, listening, and speaking, are easy to make functional. Choose tasks related to your patient's schedule, likes, dislikes, hobbies, preferences, wants, and needs. Use materials from your patient's life, such as menus, bills, and books.

Include metacognition
Treatment is most effective when your patients understand that they need it. This means that they need some awareness of their attention impairment. If a patient with mild or moderate attention impairment lacks awareness, try these steps:
- Before the task, have them predict how they'll do
- After the task, have them assess how they did
- Discuss the difference between their prediction and how they actually did
- Be encouraging as you help them identify and correct errors

When to start with worksheets

Some patients with more severe attention deficits won't be able to learn attention strategies during functional tasks. Introduce strategies with a systematic, contained task, such as a letter cancellation worksheet. For example, you teach patients to use organized scanning with a worksheet. Then, gradually work on a functional task such as reading a menu aloud.

Progressive neurological conditions

In some patients with progressive neurological conditions such as dementia, cognition will deteriorate. Attention treatment aims to maintain function for as long as possible. This requires a lot of care partner education and training (Folder et al., 2024).

Do stimulability testing for foundational strategies, such as environmental modifications and maintaining a predictable schedule. Focus your memory treatment on functional ADLs and IADLs. This can help your patient remain safe and independent for as long as possible. If you suspect that your patient has mild cognitive impairment, introduce ways to avoid/slow memory loss. Refer them to neurology for more testing and follow up (Peterson et al., 2018).

How To Do Attention Treatment

This process is for patients who have mild or mild-moderate attention impairments and some awareness of it. Use it with multi-step tasks they want to do accurately and independently, such as cooking a meal, writing an email, or paying a bill online.

General tips for attention treatment (The Center on Budget and Policy Priorities, n.d.; Cicerone et al., 2022; Weightman et al., 2014):
- Practice the task a lot.
- Focus on accuracy by giving as many cues as needed for your patient to stick to their plan.
- After the task, point out how their performance was influenced by using (or not using) their strategies.
- Encourage self-talk. Have your patients talk themselves through the task. They can also ask themselves questions to stay on track, like 'What am I doing?"

Example of attention treatment with metacognition training:

1. Do the task and reflect. After your patient completes an attention task, ask them to assess how they did.

2. Give your observations about how they did.
   ○ Be honest but encouraging. Feedback about a cognitive impairment can be hard for patients to hear. If so, put on your counseling hat and give them the time and space to express themselves.

3. Help them identify when they lost attention during the task. Give examples from the task they just did. They can ask themselves:
   ○ When did I have a hard time staying on task?
   ○ When was I doing several things at once?

4. Help them identify what they can do before a task to pay attention. For example, what steps can they take to make the task easier? They can ask themselves:
   ○ What can I do before starting a task to help me pay attention?
   ○ What can I plan ahead of time to help me stay on task?

5. Help them identify what they can do when they get off-task during the task. They can ask themselves:
    o   If I get off-task or feel overwhelmed, what can I do to help me get back on track?
    o   If I get off-task or feel overwhelmed, what's my backup plan?

6. Review the plan. Have your patient thoroughly review their plan and backup plan and look for any holes.

7. Have your patient complete the attention task again. They will monitor their own progress and accuracy.
    o   Provide as many cues as needed to remind them of their plan, backup plan, and other strategies.

8. After the task, ask your patient how they did (self-assessment).
    o   How was their accuracy and completion?
    o   How much did they stick to their plan and backup plan?
    o   How much did they self-monitor?

Review what worked and didn't work. Discuss how to adjust the plan to continue to improve.

How To Treat Working Memory

Working memory is the ability to hold information in short-term memory while doing a task. An example is remembering the step of a recipe long enough to complete it. Here are evidence-based principles for treating working memory (Cicerone et al., 2022):

- Choose working memory tasks that are functional and meaningful to the patient.
- Provide feedback and cues as needed.
- Do plenty of repetition of the working memory task.
- Systematically increase the challenge. To do this, vary:
    - The amount of information to be held in short-term memory.
    - The number of distractions present.
    - How long the information needs to be held in short-term memory.
    - How different the target information is from the distraction: More similar is harder. For example, looking for a word on a page of words is harder than looking for a word on a page of images.
    - Amount of cueing.

Functional working memory tasks:
- Spelling. Listen to a word spelled aloud, then mentally put the letters together and say the word.
- Mental math.
- Listen and repeat back. Listen to a short phrase (e.g., safety instructions, short list), then repeat it back.
- Listen and summarize. Listen to a short passage (e.g., email, paragraph from a novel) and then summarize the information.
- Listen while taking notes.
- Look then recall. Look at information and then use that information to complete a task (e.g., recipe instruction, bill total).
- Take inventory. Take inventory of things in the environment (e.g., medications to fill pill box, ingredients for a recipe).
- ADLs/IADLs while multitasking (e.g. folding laundry while answering questions).

Executive Functioning

Executive Functioning

How can you help a patient restore their executive functioning abilities? You have options! Executive functioning treatment aims to improve safety, independence, and quality of life during functional tasks. In general, use the **principles of neuroplasticity.** Repeated practice and even overlearning skills can help patients with executive dysfunction improve their safety and independence. See the Appendix to learn the principles of neuroplasticity.

Also, **use cues!** Model a skill, then ask your patient to copy you while using their strategies (i.e. self-talk). Encourage **errorless learning** by providing plenty of cues to avoid guessing. Write down and point to their strategies as a reminder to use them.

Provide counseling as needed. Your patient may first realize that they have a cognitive deficit during your speech therapy assessment. They may be shocked or even devastated. Put on your counselor hat and provide time and space for them to share their thoughts, feelings, and questions. Practice active by giving your full attention while listening, being aware of your tone and body language, repeating back what they said, and listening fully before responding (Tennant & Toney-Butler, 2023).

Refer to a mental health professional for issues with emotional regulation or mental health concerns, such as suspected anxiety or depression, that may negatively impact their quality of life.

Finally, consider **self-regulation.** Self-regulation is a significant challenge for many patients with traumatic brain injuries. They may struggle to initiate, inhibit, self-monitor, or have self-control (Kennedy & Coelho, 2005). Refer patients to a trained neuropsychologist to assess and treat self-regulation. There are evidence-based individual and group treatments that can help. As a speech therapy professional, you can still support these patients. With severe deficits, work on basic awareness, such as "I had a brain injury, and now it's hard to pay attention." For milder deficits, work on metacognition.

Teamwork

Don't go it alone! Bring in the team if your patient needs support outside your scope of practice.

- Occupational therapy for help with cognitive treatment, fine motor treatment, ADLs, and IADLs
- Physical therapy for positioning and functional mobility
- Support groups for people with strokes, brain injuries, etc.
- Neurology for help managing underlying neurological impairment
- Medical social work for community resources
- Mental health professional to address mental health needs

Use TEACH-M

TEACH-M is an acronym for a systematic way of teaching cognitive skills to patients with a traumatic brain injury or related condition. It's a good starting point for moderate to severe executive dysfunction. Here's what TEACH-M stands for and how to use it:

Task analysis
Help your patient break down the task into smaller steps. Teach them each smaller step, then 'chain' them together.

Errorless learning (Fleck & Corwin, 2013).
When teaching a new skill, focus on accuracy. Discourage guessing, model the correct answer, and give plenty of cues. If they make an error, correct it right away.

Assess performance (before, during, and after)
Assess your patient's performance before teaching a new skill. Do ongoing assessment to ensure it's the right level of challenge. Teach your patient to check their accuracy after each step of the task.

Cumulative review
Have your patient repeat all the steps of the target task, then review how they did on the task

High number of practice trials
Complete the task over and over again!

Metacognition
Help patients improve awareness about how they did on a task. Metacognition is key to improved executive functioning (Cicerone et al., 2022; Ehlhardt et al., 2005; Ehlhardt et al., 2008; Powell et al., 2012). Before the task, ask your patient to predict how they'll do. After the task, ask them to assess how they did. Discuss how their prediction compares with how they actually did.

Meaningful
We added an extra M! Meaningful treatment leads to better results.

Use Awareness Strategies

Use these strategies to help patients with mild or moderate executive functioning impairments increase self-awareness. They'll use these strategies to pause and notice how they're performing during a task. If they are aware of their errors, they're more likely to self-correct.

Give delayed feedback so patients have time to self-identify errors and self-correct. If they don't, give a nonspecific cue. "Did you do everything you needed to do?" If they still don't identify the error, provide a specific cue. "Check step 5 again."

Basic steps to improve self-awareness
- Before the task: Ask your patient to identify how they think they'll do, where they might have trouble, and possible solutions.
- During the task: The patient should do one thing at a time, pause periodically to check if they're still on task, and, if they're off-track, get back on task.
- After the task: Ask your patient to identify how they did and what they can do differently next time.

Here are self-awareness strategies (with fun acronyms!) to teach your patients:

P.A.S.E.
An acronym for Pause, Ask, Steps, Execute. Teach your patient to identify when they have stopped paying attention. Then, teach them to walk through each step of P.A.S.E. to get back on track.

- Pause. Your patient pauses their mind and body. They take a slow, deep breath.
- Ask. They take a mental step back to ask themselves: "What do I want to be doing? What's my goal?"
- Steps. They make a plan. They list the steps to accomplishing their goal.
- Execute. They follow their plan to complete the goal task.

Pause, Breathe, Return

- Pause. Your patient pauses their body and mind to identify when they're not paying attention or are feeling overwhelmed.
- Breathe. They take 3 slow, deep breaths to calm and recenter.
- Return. They bring this calm back to the task they're doing.

S.T.O.P.

The acronym STOP stands for Stop, Think, Organize, and Plan. This strategy teaches patients to notice when they've stopped paying attention and are off task.

Self-Talk (Cicerone et al., 2022)

Teach patients to talk themselves through the task. This can prevent distractions and reduce errors. When they first use self-talk with a new task, they say each step aloud to themselves. As they improve at the task, they whisper it to themselves. Finally, they use "inner speech" where they silently talk through the steps of the task inside their heads.

They can also ask themselves questions to stay on track: "What am I doing? What do I need to focus on? What else do I need to do?"

Levels of self-talk:
- Self-talk with a visual aid. Talk yourself through a task and use a visual aid (i.e. written instructions of what to do).
- Self-talk. Talk yourself through the task.
- Whisper the steps to yourself.
- Inner talk. The ultimate goal is to use inner talk, which is silently talking yourself through the steps in your head.

Executive Functioning Protocols

Goal Management Training™

If you're looking for a comprehensive executive functioning protocol, Goal Management Training (GMT) is an evidence-based option (Stamenova & Levine, 2019). It's appropriate for mild to moderate executive dysfunction. Patients learn to stop, evaluate, and then change their behaviors to achieve their goals. The program has 9 sessions that each last 1-2 hours. It can be done one-on-one or in groups.

The GMT strategy has 5 basic steps:
1. Stop
2. Define your goal
3. List the steps to attain the goal
4. Do the steps
5. Check how you did (Levine et al., 2000)

The program systematically helps patients generalize this process into their daily lives. You can learn how to get trained to administer Goal Management Training on their website (Levine et al., 2011).

Time Pressure Management (Winkens et al., 2009; Fasotti et al., 2000). Another evidence-based protocol is Time Pressure Management (TPM). TPM uses executive functioning strategies to help people with slow information processing to avoid or manage time pressure. It can improve task performance speed, efficiency, and attention.

The TPM protocol has 3 stages:
1. First, your patient identifies and accepts that they experience mental slowness.
2. Next, they learn the TPM strategy:
    ○ Analyze a task for time pressure
    ○ Make a plan
    ○ Make an emergency plan
    ○ Do the task while monitoring the results
2. Finally, they apply these strategies to daily life.

Patients learn additional strategies to manage time pressure, including asking others to repeat themselves or slow down, making a written plan before starting the task, and self-talk.

Environmental Modifications

Improving the environment can help people with executive dysfunction be safer, more comfortable, and more independent.

Remove distractions. Reduce excess noise and visual distractions (turn off the TV, shut the door)

Reduce clutter. Take down extra wall art, donate or store unnecessary items (old papers, extra furniture)
- Assign spaces for clutter (junk drawer)
- Establish clutter-free zones for workspaces

Organize the space. After reducing clutter, assign specific places for specific things (keys go on a hook by the front door)
- Set up filing systems
- Set up a message center (family calendar on the refrigerator)
- Add labels to cupboards, closets, pantry
- Use a bulletin board with labeled sections for different types of information

Use external aids. Use external aids to support executive functioning and other cognitive skills. External aids may improve organization, memory, accuracy, attention, safety, awareness, and generative thinking, to name a few (Cicerone et al., 2022; Fleck & Corwin, 2013; Jones et al., 2021; Sohlberg et al., 2007). Write down key information about schedules, routines, medications, etc. For example:
- Large family planning calendar
- File cabinets with labeled folders for home management tasks
- Post reminders of what to bring for school/work by the front door
- Reminders for how to operate appliances, like the washing machine
- Daily schedule or task schedule to help with time management
- Smartphone apps
- Calculators
- Spiral-bound notepads for notes, thoughts, and calculations
- Sticky notes, whiteboards, reminder cards
- Checklists

Functional Executive Functioning Treatment

Functional tasks are activities that patients want and need to do in their daily lives. They're meaningful and motivating, and can improve safety, independence, and quality of life.

How to know what's functional for your patient. Interview your patient and their care partner about:
- Your patient's previous level of functioning (PLOF) schedule
- Their typical schedule now
- The difference between their current and PLOF schedules
- How much help they need now vs. PLOF
- Their goals
- Their likes, dislikes, hobbies, preferences, needs, and wants

How to make executive functioning treatment functional. Do tasks that:
- They were previously able to do but can't or don't do now
- Help them reach their goals
- Are based on their likes and hobbies
- Are based on their needs and wants
- Incorporate materials from your patient's life and daily surroundings

How to make worksheets as functional as possible
- Pair worksheets with strategies your patient is stimulable for and can use after discharge. For example, your patient could use self-talk while doing an everyday math worksheet.

Patients with progressive conditions. Functional treatment is still possible for patients with progressive conditions! Goals will likely shift from increasing function to maintaining function for as long as possible.
- Educate care partners about how to support the patient
- If they have mild cognitive impairment, introduce ways to avoid memory loss

Refer to neurology if your patient doesn't have an official diagnosis but you see the signs of one.

Daily Tasks

Help your patients be more independent by working on daily tasks. Turn daily tasks into executive functioning treatment by having them:
- Set goals
- Make plans and organize
- Initiate the task and its steps
- Pay attention
- Sequence

Here's an example of how to turn a hobby into functional therapy:

1. Identify the hobby. Have your patient list their hobbies. Identify one they're having trouble doing, given their new executive functioning deficits.

2. Identify the problem. Have your patient list the steps of the hobby to help them identify which specific steps they're having trouble with.
   - For example, your patient loves to bake but stopped after their stroke. They tried recently but reported, "It didn't go well." When reviewing the steps of the task, you identify that they struggle when the recipe has more than 3 ingredients in a step.

3. Think of solutions. Help them brainstorm solutions for those tricky steps.

4. List the steps. Make a new list of all the steps of the task, including the solutions.

5. Gather the supplies. Your patient will gather the supplies they need to do the hobby. They will take inventory of what they already have and then take inventory of what they still need.
   - If supplies are missing, help them make a plan to obtain them.

6. Review the steps. Have your patient review all the steps of the task a few times.

7. Use strategies. Teach your patient to use their executive functioning strategies, such as self-talk or environmental modifications.

8   Do the task. Now do the task! Give cues and feedback as needed.

9. Review after the task. After the task, ask your patient to review how they did and what they can do differently next time. Make an updated plan to help them be more successful on the next attempt.

Other daily tasks to turn into functional treatment:
- Meeting friends: Who to invite, where, when, when to leave home to be on time.
- Grocery shopping: Meal planning, ingredients needed, budget, sales.
- Ordering at a restaurant: Reservation, menu, budget, hours of operation.
- Using public transportation: Train or bus routes and times, cost, schedule a rideshare app.
- Planning a trip: Where to go, itinerary, tickets needed, budget.
- Household chores: Supplies needed, time and energy required.

Social Communication

People with a traumatic brain injury or Right Hemisphere Disorder often have difficulties with social communication. Social communication treatment aims to improve communication in social situations (American Speech-Language-Hearing Association, n.d.j.)

Successful social communication depends on the often unspoken social conventions people are expected to follow. What these conventions are for your patient depends on their culture. Mainstream American culture, for example, encourages direct eye contact during conversation.

Other communication conventions are to:
- Listen when the other person is talking
- Not interrupt
- Take turns talking
- Stay on topic
- Let the speaker know you're listening by nodding your head, asking follow-up questions, expressing empathy, etc.

How to keep treatment culturally responsive and functional
Complete a thorough patient and care partner interview to understand their social conventions. During treatment, assess your patient's social communication based on their social conventions.

Use their daily routines to choose goal areas, such as navigating their work culture, public transportation etiquette, or small talk at a cafe.

Educate about how their verbal and nonverbal communication impacts social interactions. Educate communication partners on how to communicate with your patient more successfully. Group therapy can be an excellent way for patients to practice their social skills.

Visual Neglect

Visual Neglect

Visual neglect treatment aims to help patients better attend to and navigate their daily environments to improve safety, independence, and quality of life.

You may need to start with worksheets and other reading material to teach and practice reading and scanning strategies. The goal is to transition from worksheets to using these strategies in daily life (e.g., reading bills, eating meals, or navigating around their home).

At whatever level you start visual neglect treatment, **provide feedback.** The ultimate goal is for your patient to learn how to self-monitor their errors, so use **fading cues.** At first, give your patient enough cues to help them be successful, then gradually decrease (fade) the number of cues.

Teamwork

Don't go it alone! Bring in the team if your patient needs support outside your scope of practice (Weightman et al., 2015).
- Occupational therapy for additional visual neglect treatment and help with cognitive treatment, fine motor treatment, ADLs, and IADLs
- Physical therapy for postural support and environmental mobility and safety
- Optometrist or neuro-ophthalmologist for diagnosis, treatment of visual field cuts, prism adaptation, and other vision treatments
- Certified orientation and mobility specialist for low-vision specialty services
- Medical social work for community resources
- Mental health professionals to address mental health needs

Anchors

Add anchors as reminders to look at the affected side (Cicerone et al., 2022).

Examples of anchors:
- A strip of red tape down the affected side of the page or table.
- Numbered lines of text.
- The patient's hand resting or tapping on the affected side during a tabletop activity.
- Sensory cues. For example:
  - Tactile and visual cues: the clinician taps the patient's hand on the affected side.
  - Auditory and physical cues: the patient taps the table on the affected side.
  - Tactile cue: Velcro strip down the affected side.
- Bright sticky notes on the affected side of a computer screen.
- Bright tape on the affected side of a doorway.

Lighthouse Strategy

Ask your patient to "be a lighthouse." Their eyes and head are the light that scans the entire horizon, all the way to the left and then all the way to the right, to guide ships to safety. You can even discuss what would happen to ships if the lighthouse skipped one side of the horizon.

Use this strategy with any worksheet or reading material, from simple to complex. Then, work on scanning the environment. For example:
- Cancellation tasks
- Daily schedule tasks
- Calendar tasks
- Reading websites
- Internet navigation
- Navigating the home/building
- Typing on a keyboard
- Drawing
- Copying drawings or words
- Coloring
- Writing
- Reading supermarket ads
- Reading menus
- Locating cards or pictures on a table
- Locating functional objects such as meal items, grooming supplies, etc.
- Activities of daily living such as folding laundry, grooming, or cooking
- Playing video games!

Visual Scanning

Visual scanning is the bedrock of visual neglect treatment. It teaches patients to scan their entire visual field, from the far left to the far right. The goal is that they use visual scanning to attend to stimuli in their affected visual field (Cicerone et al., 2022; Singh, 2023; Weightman et al., 2014)

Common visual scanning treatment tasks include:
- Cancellation tasks
- Picture description
- Reading: from single letters spread over a page to reading phrases, sentences, paragraphs, then pages
- Writing: from writing single letters to writing pages of information

Reading Strategies

Help your patient be as successful as possible by giving plenty of cues and prompts to use their visual neglect strategies when reading. As your patient improves, gradually fade cues and work on increasing self-awareness of their visual neglect (Blake et al., 2016; Cicerone et al. 2022).

To make a reading task easier:
- Use larger fonts (size 24 or larger).
- Use shorter reading material, such as words or sentences.
- Present only 1 target at a time.
- Add space between targets.
- Add numbers to both sides of the page as anchors.
- Use less visually complex targets, such as simple black-and-white line drawings.
- Slow down reading speed by having your patient read aloud or touch each word.

To increase generalization:
- Use standard-sized fonts (size 12).
- Use longer and more functional reading material, such as paragraphs or pages from a book.
- Present multiple targets.
- Use more visually complex targets, such as color photos with captions in a magazine.

Mental Imagery Training

Visuomotor mental imagery training may help patients improve attention to the affected side of their visual field.

Mental imagery treatment can include:
- Visualizing the space of their visual deficit. They close their eyes and think about what they should be seeing (Smania et al., 1997)
- Closing their eyes and describing a familiar place in detail, especially the affected side.

Contralateral Limb Activation

Contralateral limb activation is applying stimuli to the affected side of the body. In other words, the limb is 'contralateral' (on the opposite side of the brain damage (Beis et al., 2004). For most patients with visual neglect, this means applying stimuli to their left side. The goal is that this stimulation will help the damaged hemisphere of the brain heal and improve attention to the affected side.

Your patient "activates" the contralateral limb by doing many repetitive motions with that limb.

For example:
- Tap with the affected-side hand or foot
- Clench and unclench their affected hand
- Lift their affected shoulder
- Squeeze a stress ball
- TENS unit electrodes or vibration on the affected side can also deliver stimuli

Your patient can pair limb activation with a functional task, like reading.

Contralateral limb activation protocol for left visual neglect when reading left to right (Cicerone et al., 2022):

1. Your patient places their left hand on the far left of the reading material. They tap their left hand repeatedly.

2. They look at their tapping left hand to find the beginning of the line.

3. They read the line.

4. They prompt themselves to "scan to my hand."

5. If they lose their place, they prompt themselves to "move my left hand" to find it.

6. Continue activating the affected side as needed while reading.

Environmental Modifications

Environmental modifications can help people with visual neglect be safer more comfortable, and more independent.

Safety
- Put painter's tape or reflective tape in a contrasting color on the edges of doorways, steps, and thresholds. For example, place white reflective tape on dark steps.
- Wear non-skid shoes or slippers in the home.
- Remove rugs and runners or add non-slip backing.
- Post safety signs ("Step").

Add anchors to the affected side (Cicerone et al., 2022). Anchors are reminders to look at the affected side. Examples are bright notes on the side of a computer screen or a line of red tape down the side of a table.

Improve lighting and visuals
- Add lighting to dark spaces. Avoid glare (cover reflective surfaces).
- Increase contrast (e.g. a dark placemat under a white plate).

Reduce clutter
- Declutter to remove distractions and improve safety.
- Arrange furniture to make straight walking paths and open spaces.

Organize the space
- Keep items in the same place so they're easier to find.
- Organize items into labeled bins, folders, and drawers.

Use the affected side to encourage attention to that side
- Have communication partners sit on the affected side.
- Have objects of interest (window, TV) on the affected side.

Use the 'good' side to improve safety. Sit or place important items on the person's unaffected side:
- Food and drink to ensure adequate nutrition and hydration.
- Medications.
- Important papers.
- Whenever the person is tired.

Appendix

Principles of Neuroplasticity

Neuroplasticity is the central nervous system's ability to reorganize and make new connections in response to experiences. The 10 principles of neuroplasticity (as outlined by Kleim and Jones, 2008) are "highlights" of the factors most relevant to brain damage recovery.

Keep these principles of neuroplasticity in mind when making treatment plans.

1. **Use it or lose it.** Function can be lost if the associated part of the brain isn't activated.

2. **Use it and improve it.** The more you practice a specific brain function, the more that function will improve.

3. **Specificity matters.** Brain changes (such as new connections and reorganization) occur in the parts of the brain that are being used during an action, so keep treatment functional for your patient. For example, do swallowing exercises to treat dysphagia and choose vocabulary your patient frequently uses to treat aphasia.

4. **Repetition matters.** Remember that behavioral changes occur before brain changes, so repeat an action often and over an extended period of time.

5. **Intensity matters.** To induce neuroplasticity, a certain high threshold of intensity (e.g., length of exercise, number of sessions) must be reached.

Choose the right level of intensity based on your patients' unique factors. High-intensity treatment may be contraindicated for patients in the very acute post brain injury phase. Once they are medically stable, higher-intensity training is shown to lead to better results. For patients with ALS, MS, and other neurodegenerative conditions, that threshold of intensity may be modified or avoided entirely.

6. **Time matters.** Spending enough time on treatment is required for brain changes to be stable and long-lasting. For acquired brain injuries, neuronal changes are more likely to happen during the

early, spontaneous recovery period, while other changes happen over weeks and months of consistent training.

7. **Salience matters.** The function being treated must be meaningful to your patient to maximize neuroplasticity. In other words, keep treatment functional and meaningful! Interview your patient. What matters to them? What motivates them? Incorporate these in your treatment plan.

8. **Age matters.** Although younger brains have more neuroplasticity, older brains can still change, although at a slower rate.

Encourage a healthy lifestyle to slow down the effects of aging. A healthy lifestyle includes eating right, physical exercise, good-quality sleep, mental exercise, and socializing. Be aware of age-related changes that impact neuroplasticity. For example, decreased oral sensory awareness may result in compensations in the older brain.

9. **Transference.** Neuroplasticity from one training experience (e.g. loud speech) can sometimes transfer to or enhance related skills (swallowing).

Enrich the environment as appropriate. Patients with visual neglect, for example, may benefit from bright painter's tape and sticky notes that direct attention to their neglected side. While patients with dementia benefit from fewer visual and auditory distractions.

10. **Interference.** Not all neuroplasticity is desirable. For example, compensatory behaviors can interfere with the desired function.

Encourage patients to nip "bad habits" that undermine their progress in the bud. An example of this is over-relying on a care partner. Find ways to incorporate practice of the desired function into a patient's daily routine.

Motor Learning

The goal of motor learning is to help your patient learn and retain new movements. See the following chart for a one-page summary of how to use the principles of motor learning in your practice.

Use pre-practice

Set your patient up for success before starting motor treatment. Take the time to make sure that your patient:

- Is motivated. Speech therapy treatment can be tough. Being motivated can help your patient stay focused on their goals.
- Understands the expectations of your treatment (what a "correct" response is and why).
- Is stimulable for the treatment you choose. Test to see whether they can do the movement, respond to certain cues, etc.

Use a large number of trials

Practicing a movement over and over leads to superior learning of that movement. Aim for at least 50 repetitions per target.

How you structure all of this practice also makes a difference in motor learning:

Distributed and massed practice

Distributed practice is a longer duration of therapy with fewer sessions per week. Massed practice is a shorter duration of therapy with more sessions per week. For example, your patient has 20 sessions of therapy. With distributed practice, you schedule 2 sessions per week for 10 weeks. With massed practice, the schedule may be 4 sessions per week for 5 weeks.

Rehab-therapy research suggests that distributed practice is best for motor learning (Maas et al., 2008). Our work schedules often already use this type of practice, for example, seeing a patient 2-3x per week.

That said, research shows that massed practice is also effective for some patients (Wambaugh et al., 2013; Maas et al., 2008). The takeaway is that motor therapy helps, even if you can't offer an intensive schedule.

Variable and constant practice.

Variable practice is practicing a movement in different ways. For example, practicing several different phonemes in different word positions.

Constant practice is practicing the same movement over and over again. For example, practicing one phoneme in the same word position.

To learn a movement, use constant practice. To retain a movement, use variable practice.

For example, your new patient practices one phoneme in word-initial position (constant practice), and then she practices a 2nd phoneme in word-initial position. Once she has reached a certain level of accuracy with those movements, she moves on to practice both phonemes in word-initial and final positions (variable practice).

Random and blocked practice

Random practice (versus blocked) is practicing movements throughout the session in random order. For example, your patient practices both /f/ and /z/ in random order throughout an entire session. Blocked practice is practicing one movement first, then moving on to practice another movement. You 'block' out each movement. For example, you practice /f/ for the first half of a session and then /z/ for the rest of the session.

Start with blocked practice to learn the movement. In the early stages of treatment or with severe impairment, a patient may need to practice each target individually to learn them (/f/ for the first half of the session, /z/ for the final half). Once they've reached a certain level of accuracy, they can move on to random practice of these phonemes (Wambaugh et al., 2014; Knock et al., 2000; Maas et al., 2008).

Complex and simple practice

Complex refers to the whole movement, the sum of all its parts. For example, saying a multisyllabic word is a complex movement, while saying an individual phoneme in that word is a simple movement.

Practicing a complex movement can improve motor learning of both complex **and** simple movements. And some evidence suggests that complex movements better improve motor learning for patients with apraxia of speech (Maas et al., 2002).

The research is mixed on which is better for motor learning as a whole. It may depend on the movement being learned. For example, if the parts of a complex movement are easy to separate out, practicing those parts (simple movements) may be beneficial (Maas et al., 2008).

Feedback: Knowledge of performance and results

Knowledge of performance is specific feedback ("Bring your lips closer together for that sound"). This kind of feedback is better when a movement is new or unfamiliar.

Knowledge of results is feedback about whether the movement was done right or wrong ("Not quite"). This type of feedback is best to help patients retain the movement.

Feedback: Frequent and reduced

Frequent feedback is giving feedback after every attempt of the movement. In the early stages of treatment, frequent feedback can help patients learn the new movement (Bislick et al., 2012).

Reduced feedback is when you don't give feedback every single time your patient tries a movement. Instead, you reduce your feedback to, for example, every other movement or every 5 movements (50% or 20%).

Reduced feedback helps patients self-monitor as they practice movements. Less feedback teaches them how to detect their mistakes instead of depending on the clinician to point them out. This improves motor learning. When given reduced feedback, patients with apraxia of speech and dysarthria have higher retention of motor learning than those given frequent feedback. Their movement performance may be lower during the session, but retention (or motor learning) is higher.

Feedback: Immediate and delayed

Immediate feedback is when you give feedback right after your patient does a movement. This may help them learn how to do a new movement.

Delayed feedback is when you pause first. For example, wait 5 seconds after the trial before giving feedback. This gives your patient enough time to evaluate their own performance. This type of feedback improves motor learning.

(Bislick, n.d.)

To First Learn A Movement	For Motor Learning
Constant practice	**Variable practice**
• Practice the same movement a lot • For example, practice one phoneme in the same word position	• Practice a movement in different ways • For example, practice several different phonemes in different word positions
Blocked practice	**Random practice**
• Practice one movement first, then practice the next movement • For example, practice /f/ the first half of a session and then /z/ the second half of a session	• Practice movements in random order throughout a session • For example, practice /f/ and /z/ in random order throughout a session
Knowledge of performance	**Knowledge of results**
• Give feedback about how to do the movement • For example, "Bring your lips closer together for that sound"	• Give feedback about whether they did the movement right or wrong • For example, "Not quite," or, "That was clear"
Frequent, immediate feedback	**Reduced, delayed feedback**
• Give feedback after every attempt • Give feedback right away	• Give feedback every few attempts • Wait a few seconds before giving feedback

(Bislick, n.d; Bislick et al., 2012; Knock et al., 2000; Mass et al., 2002; Mass et al., 2008; Park et al., 2016; Wambaugh et al. 2013; Wambaugh et al., 2014)

Modify Tasks

The "just right" challenge means a task is challenging but still doable for your patient. What's "just right" can change from session to session or even within a session. Use cues and prompts to modify tasks and also try the following:

To make tasks easier:
- Remove distractions
- Give 2+ choices for the correct answer
- Use simple sentence structure
- Use fading cues. Start with frequent and more detailed cues. Gradually fade to occasional and general cues
- Remind your patient to use their strategies
- Make the task meaningful or motivating

To make tasks harder:
- Add distractors
- Add more choices
- Ask open-ended questions
- Include more complex sentence structure
- Continue to use meaningful or motivating tasks!

There's only so much you can do to make a task the just-right challenge. Consider whether other factors are impacting your patient's performance:

- Physiological factors, such as issues with sleep, nutrition, medication side effects, pain, comorbidities, etc. (National Institute on Aging, 2020)
- Psychological factors, such as depression or stress
- Patient's motivation
- Socio-economic factors, such as lack of help at home, lack of transportation, financial constraints, etc.

Refer to other disciplines, such as occupational therapy, physical therapy, social work, or nursing, so they can help follow up with these factors.

Differential Diagnosis for Apraxia, Dysarthria, and Aphasia

Characteristic	Apraxia	Dysarthria	Aphasia
Distorted sound substitutions & additions (not including intrusive schwa "uh")	✓	-	-
Inaccurate speech AMRs ("puhpuhpuh")	✓	-	-
Speech SMRs ("puhtuhkuh") more difficult than AMRs	✓	-	✓
Increased sound distortions/ distorted sound substitutions with increased speech rate, utterance length, &/or complexity	✓	-	-
Reduced words per breath group relative to max. vowel duration	✓	-	-
Muscle weakness	-	✓	-
Respiration affected	-	✓	-
Phonation affected	-	✓	-
Resonance affected	-	✓	-
Voice changes	-	✓	-
Language processing deficits	-	-	✓
Reading and/or writing abilities affected	-	-	✓
Articulatory deficits	✓	✓	-
Prosodic deficits	✓	✓	-
Sound distortions	✓	✓	-
Slow overall speech rate	✓	✓	-
Lengthened intersegment durations	✓	✓	-
Lengthened vowel and/or consonant segments	✓	✓	-
Syllable segmentation within/across words in phrases/sentences	✓	✓	-
Articulatory groping	✓	-	-
Inconsistent errors	✓	-	✓
Sound/syllable repetitions	✓	✓	✓
Sound prolongations	✓	✓	✓

(Strand et al., 2014)

References

1. Affoo, R.H., & Hachey, S. (2022). Integrating Oral Health in Speech-Language Pathology Practice: A Viewpoint. Perspectives of the ASHA Special Interest Group, 7(3), 868-878. https://doi.org/10.1044/2022_PERSP-21-00277

2. Aguirre, E., Woods, R. T., Spector, A., & Orrell, M. (2013). Cognitive stimulation for dementia: A systematic review of the evidence of effectiveness from randomised controlled trials. Ageing Research Reviews, 12(1), 253-262. https://doi.org/10.1016/j.arr.2012.07.001

3. Allison, K.M., Cordella, C., Iuzzini-Seigel, J., & Green, J.R. (2020). Differential Diagnosis of Apraxia of Speech in Children and Adults: A Scoping Review. Journal of speech, language, and hearing research, 63(9), 2952–2994. https://doi.org/10.1044/2020_JSLHR-20-00061

4. ALS Association: Minnesota, North Dakota, South Dakota Chapter. (n.d.). Adaptive Equipment. The ALS Association. Retrieved September, 2024, from https://www.als.org/sites/default/files/2021-01/Adaptive_Equipment_Listing.pdf

5. Alzheimer's Association. (n.d.). Daily Care Plan. Retrieved April, 2024, from https://www.alz.org/help-support/caregiving/daily-care/daily-care-plan

6. American Speech-Language Hearing Association. (n.d.). Voice Disorders. Practice Portal. Retrieved 2022, from www.asha.org/Practice-Portal/Clinical-Topics/Voice-Disorders

7. American Speech-Language-Hearing Association. (n.d.). Right Hemisphere Damage. [Practice Portal]. www.asha.org/Practice-Portal/Clinical-Topics/Right-Hemisphere-Damage

8. American Speech-Language-Hearing Association. (n.d.). Acquired Apraxia of Speech. [Practice Portal]. www.asha.org/practice-portal/clinical-topics/acquired-apraxia-of-speech

9. American Speech-Language-Hearing Association. (n.d.). Adult Dysphagia. Practice Portal. Retrieved October, 2024, from www.asha.org/Practice-Portal/Clinical-Topics/Adult-Dysphagia/

10. American Speech-Language-Hearing Association. (n.d.). Dementia. [Practice Portal]. Retrieved August, 2023, from www.asha.org/Practice-Portal/Clinical-Topics/Dementia

11. American Speech-Language-Hearing Association. (n.d.). Distinguishing Perceptual Characteristics and Physiologic Findings by Dysarthria Type. Retrieved March, 2024, from https://www.asha.org/practice-portal/clinical-topics/dysarthria-in-adults/distinguishing-perceptual-characteristics/

12. American Speech-Language-Hearing Association. (n.d.). Dysarthria in adults. [Practice Portal]. Retrieved Sept, 2023, from https://www.asha.org/practice-portal/clinical-topics/dysarthria-in-adults/

13. American Speech-Language-Hearing Association. (n.d.). Fluency Disorders. Practice Portal. Retrieved September, 2024, from www.asha.org/practice-portal/clinical-topics/fluency-disorders

14. American Speech-Language-Hearing Association. (n.d.). Head and neck cancer [Practice portal]. Retrieved September, 2024, from https://www.asha.org/Practice-Portal/Clinical-Topics/Head-and-Neck-Cancer

15. American Speech-Language-Hearing Association. (n.d.). Social communication disorder. [Practice portal]. Retrieved October, 2024, from www.asha.org/Practice-Portal/Clinical-Topics/Social-Communication-Disorder/

16. American Speech-Language-Hearing Association. (n.d.). Resonance disorders [Practice portal]. Retrieved February, 2025, from https://www.asha.org/Practice-Portal/Clinical-Topics/Resonance-Disorders/

17. American Speech-Language-Hearing Association-2 (n.d.) Flexible Endoscopic Evaluation of Swallowing (FEES). Retrieved May, 3, 2024 from https://www.asha.org/practice-portal/clinical-topics/pediatric-feeding-and-swallowing/flexible-endoscopic-evaluation-of-swallowing/

18. American Speech-Language-Hearing Association-3 (n.d.) Videofluoroscopic Swallow Study (VFSS). Retrieved May 3, 2024 from https://www.asha.org/practice-portal/clinical-topics/pediatric-feeding-and-swallowing/videofluoroscopic-swallow-study/

19. Angadi, V., Croake, D., & Stemple, J. (2019). Effects of Vocal Function Exercises: A Systematic Review. Journal of voice : official journal of the Voice Foundation, 33(1), 124.e13–124.e34. https://doi.org/10.1016/j.jvoice.2017.08.031

20. Aparo, M., Brewer, C., & Kleindel, A. (n.d.) Adult Speech Therapy. [Website]. https://adultspeechtherapy.co

21. Aphasia Institute. (n.d.). Communication Tools: Communicative Access & Supported Conversation for Adults With Aphasia (SCA™) – Aphasia Institute. Aphasia Institute. Retrieved Dec 19, 2023, from https://www.aphasia.ca/communication-tools-communicative-access-sca/

22. Aspire Products LLC. (n.d.). Precautions and contraindications. emst150.com. Retrieved October, 2024, from https://emst150.com/wp-content/uploads/2021/03/Contraindications-11-2019.pdf

23. Aviv, J. (2017). The Acid Watcher Diet: A 28-Day Reflux Prevention and Healing Program. Harmony/Rodale.

24. Azouvi, P., Marchal, F., Samuel, C., Morin, L., Renard, C., Louis-Dreyfus, A., Jokie, C., Wiart, L., Pradat-Diehl, P., Deloche, G., & Bergego, C. (1996). Functional consequences and awareness of unilateral neglect: Study of an evaluation scale. Neuropsychological Rehabilitation, 6(2), 133-150. https://doi.org/10.1080/713755501

25. Azouvi, P., Olivier, S., de Montety, G., Samuel, C., Louis-Dreyfus, A., & Tesio, L. (2003). Behavioral assessment of unilateral neglect: study of the psychometric properties of the Catherine Bergego Scale. Archives of physical medicine and rehabilitation, 84(1), 51-57. https://doi.org/10.1053/apmr.2003.50062

26. Bahia, M.M., & Lowell, S.Y. (2020). A Systematic Review of the Physiological Effects of the Effortful Swallow Maneuver in Adults With Normal and Disordered Swallowing. American journal of speech-language pathology, 29(3), 1655–1673. https://doi.org/10.1044/2020_AJSLP-19-00132

27. Balou, M., Herzberg, E.G., Kamelhar, D., & Molfenter, S.M. (2019). An intensive swallowing exercise protocol for improving swallowing physiology in older adults with radiographically confirmed dysphagia. Clinical interventions in aging, 14, 283–288. https://doi.org/10.2147/CIA.S194723

28. Barnes, G. (n.d.). Breathing and Eating: Can My Patient Eat After a Trach or Vent? Part 2 [Recorded Webinar]. Medbridge Education. https://www.medbridge.com/courses/details/breathing-and-eating-can-my-patient-eat-after-a-trach-or-vent-part-2-recorded-webinar-george-barnes

29. Beeke, S., Sirman, N., Beckley, F., Maxim, J., Edwards, S., Swinburn, K., & Best, W. (2013). Better Conversations with Aphasia: an e-learning resource. https://extend.ucl.ac.uk/

30. Beilby, J.M., Byrnes, M.L., & Yaruss, J.S. (2012). Acceptance and Commitment Therapy for adults who stutter: psychosocial adjustment and speech fluency. Journal of fluency disorders, 37(4), 289–299. https://doi.org/10.1016/j.jfludis.2012.05.003

31. Beis, J.M., Keller, C., Morin, N., Bartolomeo, P., Bernati, T., Chokron, S., Leclercq, M., Louis-Dreyfus, A., Marchal, F., Martin, Y., Perennou, D., Pradat-Diehl, P., Prairial, C., Rode, G., Rousseaux, M., Samuel, C., Sieroff, E., Wiart, L., Azouvi, P., & French Collaborative Study Group on Assessment of Unilateral Neglect. (2004). Right spatial neglect after left hemisphere stroke: qualitative and quantitative study. Neurology, 63(9), 1600-1605. https://doi.org/10.1212/01.wnl.0000142967.60579.32

32. Benigas, J.E. (n.d.). External Memory Aids and Memory Books for Memory Loss [Online course]. Medbridge. https://www.medbridge.com/educate/courses/external-memory-aids-and-memory-books-for-memory-loss-jeanette-benigas

33. Benigas, J.E. (n.d.). Spaced retrieval for memory loss part 1: screenings, development, and support. Medbridge. https://www.medbridgeeducation.com/courses/details/spaced-retrieval-for-memory-loss-part-1-screenings-development-and-support-jeanette-benigas

34. Benigas, J.E. (n.d.). Spaced retrieval for memory loss part 2: implementation strategies. https://www.medbridge.com/course-catalog/details/spaced-retrieval-for-memory-loss-part-2-implementation-strategies-jeanette-benigas/.

35. Beukelman, D., Fager, S., & Nordness, A. (2011). Communication Support for People with ALS. Neurology research international, 2011, 714693. https://doi.org/10.1155/2011/714693

36. Beukelman, D. R., Garrett, K. L., & Yorkston, K. M. (2007). *Augmentative Communication Strategies for Adults with Acute Or Chronic Medical Conditions*. Paul H. Brookes Publishing Company.

37. Beukelman, D.R., & Mirenda, P. (2012). Augmentative and alternative communication: Supporting children and adults with complex communication needs. Brookes Publishing.

38. Bier, J., Hazarian, L., McCabe, D., & Perez, Y. (2004). Giving your patient a voice with a tracheostomy speaking valve. Nursing, 34, Suppl: 16-18. https://doi.org/10.1097/00152193-200410001-00005

39. Bislick, L. (n.d.). Principles of Motor Learning and Motor Speech Disorders [Online course]. Medbridge. Retrieved 2021, from https://www.medbridge.com/course-catalog/details/principles-of-motor-learning-and-motor-speech-disorders-lauren-bislick-slp/

40. Bislick, L.P., Weir, P.C., Spencer, K., Kendall, D., & Yorkston, K.M. (2012). Do principles of motor learning enhance retention and transfer of speech skills? A systematic review. Aphasiology, 26(5), 709-728. https://doi.org/10.1080/02687038.2012.676888

41. Blake, M., Novak, K., & Freer, J. (2016). Treatment Strategies for Unilateral Visuospatial Neglect and Anosognosia. Retrieved from https://www.medbridgeeducation.com/blog/2016/02/treatment-strategies-for-unilateral-neglectand-anosognosia/

42. Bogdanova, Y., Yee, M. K., Ho, V. T., & Cicerone, K. D. (2016). Computerized Cognitive Rehabilitation of Attention and Executive Function in Acquired Brain Injury: A Systematic Review. *The Journal of head trauma rehabilitation*, 31(6), 419–433. https://doi.org/10.1097/HTR.0000000000000203

43. Boone, D.R., & McFarlane, S.C. (1993). A critical view of the yawn-sigh as a voice therapy technique. Journal of voice : official journal of the Voice Foundation, 7(1), 75-80. https://doi.org/10.1016/s0892-1997(05)80114-6

44. Bourgeois, M. (2015). Innovative treatments for persons with dementia [Online Video]. ASHA Clinical Research Education Library. https://academy.pubs.asha.org/2015/11/innovative-treatments-for-persons-with-dementia/

45. Boyle, M. (n.d.) Semantic feature analysis treatment for individuals with aphasia. Medbridge. https://www.medbridgeeducation.com/courses/details/semantic-feature-analysis-treatment-for-individuals-with-aphasia-mary-boyle-aphasia

46. Boyle, M. (2010). Semantic feature analysis treatment for aphasic word retrieval impairments: what's in a name? Topics in stroke rehabilitation, 17(6), 411-422. https://doi.org/10.1310/tsr1706-411.

47. Boyle, M.P. (2018). Disclosing Stuttering: How is it done and what are the effects? American Institute for Stuttering. Retrieved October, 2024, from https://www.stutteringtreatment.org/blog/disclosing-stuttering-how-is-it-done-and-what-are-the-effects

48. Boyle, M.P., Milewski, K.M., & Beita-Ell, C. (2018). Disclosure of stuttering and quality of life in people who stutter. Journal of Fluency Disorders, 58, 1-10. https://doi.org/10.1016/j.jfludis.2018.10.003

49. Brewer, C. (2023). The Adult Speech Therapy Roadmap [online course]. https://theadultspeechtherapyroadmap.mykajabi.com/

50. Brignell, A., Krahe, M., Downes, M., Kefalianos, E., Reilly, S., & Morgan, A. T. (2020). A systematic review of interventions for adults who stutter. Journal of Fluency Disorders, 64(2020), 1-18. https://doi.org/10.1016/j.jfludis.2020.105766

51. Broadhouse, K.M., Singh, M.F., Suo, C., Gates, N., Wen, W., Brodaty, H., Jain, N., Wilson, G.C., Meiklejohn, J., Singh, N., Baune, B.T., Baker, M., Foroughi, N., Wang, Y., Kochan, N., Ashton, K., Brown, M., Li, Z., Mavros, Y., ... Valenzuela, M.J.

(2020). Hippocampal plasticity underpins long-term cognitive gains from resistance exercise in MCI. NeuroImage. Clinical, 25, 102182. https://doi.org/10.1016/j.nicl.2020.102182

52. Brownlee, A. (2021). Communication Options for People with ALS. The ALS Association. https://www.als.org/sites/default/files/2021-04/Communication%20Options%20for%20People%20With%20ALS.pdf

53. Brownlee, A. (2021). DME and Assistive Technology That Helps Caregivers. The ALS Association. Retrieved August, 2024, from https://www.als.org/sites/default/files/2021-11/DME-and-AT_0.pdf

54. Brundage, S.B., Ratner, N.B., Boyle, M.P., Eggers, K., Everard, R., Franken, M.C., Kefalianos, E., Marcotte, A.K., Millard, S., Packman, A., Vanryckeghem, M., & Yaruss, J.S. (2021). Consensus Guidelines for the Assessments of Individuals Who Stutter Across the Lifespan. American journal of speech-language pathology, 30(6), 2379–2393. https://doi.org/10.1044/2021_AJSLP-21-00107

55. Brush, J. (2018). Tips for Creating Signs. Brush Development. Retrieved April, 2024, from https://brushdevelopment.com/tips-creating-signs

56. Brush, J., & Bourgeois, M. (2020). Montessori Developmental Principles to Support the Needs of the Elderly. *Association Montessori Internationale*. https://doi.org/2020

57. Brush, J., Fleder, H., & Calkins, M. (2012). Using the Environment to Support Communication and Foster Independence in People with Dementia: A review of case studies in long term care settings. Brush Development. Retrieved April, 2024, from https://brushdevelopment.com/wp-content/uploads/2015/09/IDEAS_publication_may2012.pdf

58. Bunker, L.D., Nessler, C., & Wambaugh, J.L. (2019). Effect Size Benchmarks for Response Elaboration Training: A Meta-Analysis. American journal of speech-language pathology, 28(1S), 247–258. https://doi.org/10.1044/2018_AJSLP-17-0152

59. Burton, B., Isaacs, M., Brogan, E., Shrubsole, K., Kilkenny, M.F., Power, E., Godecke, E., Cadilhac, D., Copland, A., & Wallace, S.J. (2023). An updated systematic review of stroke clinical practice guidelines to inform aphasia management. International journal of stroke : official journal of the International Stroke Society, 18(9), 1029–1039. https://doi.org/10.1177/17474930231161454

60. Cahill, L.M., Turner, A.B., Stabler, P.A., Addis, P.E., Theodoros, D.G., & Murdoch, B.E. (2004). An evaluation of continuous positive airway pressure (CPAP) therapy in the treatment of hypernasality following traumatic brain injury: A report of 3 cases. The Journal of Head Trauma Rehabilitation, 19(3), 241–253. https://doi.org/10.1097/00001199-200405000-00005

61. Caute, A., Pring, T., Cocks, N., Cruice, M., Best, W., & Marshall, J. (2013). Enhancing communication through gesture and naming therapy. Journal of Speech, Language, and Hearing Research, 56(1), 337-351. https://doi.org/10924388005600010337

62. Cedars-Sinai. (2018). Esophagitis Diet (Soft Food) Guidelines. Cedars-Sinai. Retrieved September, 2024, from https://www.cedars-sinai.org/blog/esophageal-soft-diet-guidelines.html

63. Chen, H.J., Chen, J.L., Chen, C.Y., Lee, M., Chang, W.H., & Huang, T.T. (2019). Effect of an Oral Health Programme on Oral Health, Oral Intake, and Nutrition in Patients with Stroke and Dysphagia in Taiwan: A Randomised Controlled Trial. International journal of environmental research and public health, 16(12), 2228. https://doi.org/10.3390/ijerph16122228

64. Chipps, E., Gatens, C., Genter, L., Musto, M., Dubis-Bohn, A., Gliemmo, M., Dudley, K., Holloman, C., Hoet, A. E., & Landers, T. (2014). Pilot study of an oral care protocol on poststroke survivors. Rehabilitation nursing : the official journal of the Association of Rehabilitation Nurses, 39(6), 294-304. https://doi.org/10.1002/rnj.154

65. Chiu, H.Y., Chen, P.Y., Chen, Y.T., & Huang, H.C. (2018). Reality orientation therapy benefits cognition in older people with dementia: A meta-analysis. International journal of nursing studies, 86, 20-28. https://doi.org/10.1016/j.ijnurstu.2018.06.008

66. Cicerone, K. D., Dams-O'Connor, K., Eberle, R., Fraas, M., Ganci, K., Langenbahn, D., Shapiro-Rosenbaum, A., Tate, R. L., Trexler, L. E., & ACRM | American Congress Of Rehabilitation Medicine. (2022). ACRM Cognitive Rehabilitation Manual & Textbook Second Edition: Translating Evidence-Based Recommendations Into Practice (R. Eberle, A. Shapiro-Rosenbaum, & ACRM | American Congress Of Rehabilitation Medicine, Eds.). ACRM.

67. Cleveland Clinic. (2020). Improving Communication in Patients with Parkinson's Disease. Cleveland Clinic. Retrieved October, 2024, from https://my.clevelandclinic.org/health/diseases/9392-speech-therapy-for-parkinsons-disease

68. Costello, J. M. (2016). Message Banking, Voice Banking and Legacy Messages. Boston Children's Hospital.

69. Costello, J., & OBrien, M. (n.d.). Speech and augmentative alternative communication AAC in ALS. Medbridge. https://www.medbridge.com/courses/details/speech-and-augmentative-alternative-communication-aac-in-als-john-costello-meghan-obrien

70. Crispiatico, V., Baldanzi, C., Napoletano, A., Tomasoni, L., Tedeschi, F., Groppo, E., Rovaris, M., Vitali, C., & Cattaneo, D. (2021). Effects of voice rehabilitation in people with MS: A double-blinded long-term randomized controlled trial. Multiple sclerosis (Houndmills, Basingstoke, England), 28(7), 1081-1090. https://doi.org/10.1177/13524585211051059

71. Crosson, B. (2008). An intention manipulation to change lateralization of word production in nonfluent aphasia: current status. Seminars in speech and language, 29(3), 188–200. https://doi.org/10.1055/s-0028-1082883

72. Davis, G.A. (1980). *A Critical Look at PACE Therapy*. Clinical Aphasiology: Proceeding of the Conference 1980 [Presentation].

73. Dawson, P., & Guare, R. (n.d.). Definition of Terms. Smart But Scattered Kids. Retrieved August, 2024, from https://www.smartbutscatteredkids.com/about/terms/

74. de Swart, B.J.M., Willemse, S.C., Maassen, B.A.M., & Horstink, M.W.I.M. (2003). Improvement of voicing in patients with Parkinson's disease by speech therapy. Neurology, 60(3), 498-500. https://doi.org/10.1212/01.WNL.0000044480.95458.56

75. Dehqan, A., & Scherer, R. C. (2019). Positive Effects of Manual Circumlaryngeal Therapy in the Treatment of Muscle Tension Dysphonia (MTD): Long Term Treatment Outcomes. *Journal of voice : official journal of the Voice Foundation, 33*(6), 866–871. https://doi.org/10.1016/j.jvoice.2018.07.010

76. Desjardins, M., & Bonilha, H.S. (2020). The Impact of Respiratory Exercises on Voice Outcomes: A Systematic Review of the Literature. Journal of voice : official journal of the Voice Foundation, 34(4), 648.e1–648.e39. https://doi.org/10.1016/j.jvoice.2019.01.011

77. Desjardins, M., Halstead, L., Simpson, A., Flume, P., & Bonilha, H.S. (2022). Respiratory Muscle Strength Training to Improve Vocal Function in Patients with Presbyphonia. Journal of voice : official journal of the Voice Foundation, 36(3), 344–360. https://doi.org/10.1016/j.jvoice.2020.06.006

78. DeVore, K., & Cookman, S. (2020). The Voice Book: Caring For, Protecting, and Improving Your Voice. Chicago Review Press.

79. Dictionary.com, LLC. (n.d.). Meanings & Definitions of English Words. Dictionary.com. Retrieved October, 2024, from https://www.dictionary.com/

80. Dietz, A. (2014). Supported Reading Comprehension for People with Aphasia: Visual and Linguistic Supports. Journal of Medical Speech-language Pathology, 21(4), 319-331.

81. Duffy, J. R. (2013). Motor Speech Disorders: Substrates, Differential Diagnosis, and Management. Elsevier Mosby.

82. Duffy, J.R. (2020). Motor speech disorders: Substrates, differential diagnosis, and management (4th ed.). Elsevier.

83. Ebihara, T., Ebihara, S., Watando, A., Okazaki, T., Asada, M., Ohrui, T., Yamaya, M., & Arai, H. (2006). Effects of menthol on the triggering of the swallowing reflex in elderly patients with dysphagia. *British Journal of Clinical Pharmacology, 62*(3), 369-371. https://doi.org/10.1111/j.1365-2125.2006.02666.x

84. Edmonds, L. (n.d.). VNeST Protocols: Cases, Assessment, and Outcome Measures [Online Course]. Medbridge. https://www.medbridge.com/course-catalog/details/VNeST-protocols-cases-assessment-and-outcome-measures-lisa-a-edmonds-aphasia

85. Edmonds, L.A., Nadeau, S.E., & Kiran, S. (2009). Effect of Verb Network Strengthening Treatment (VNeST) on Lexical Retrieval of Content Words in Sentences in Persons with Aphasia. Aphasiology, 23(3), 402–424. https://doi.org/10.1080/02687030802291339

86. Efstratiadou, E.A., Papathanasiou, I., Holland, R., Archonti, A., & Hilari, K. (2018). Systematic Review of Semantic Feature Analysis Therapy Studies for Aphasia. Journal of speech, language, and hearing research : JSLHR, 61(5), 1261–1278. https://doi.org/10.1044/2018_JSLHR-L-16-0330

87. Ehlhardt, L.A., Sohlberg, M.M., Glang, A., & Albin, R. (2005). TEACH-M: A pilot study evaluating an instructional sequence for persons with impaired memory and executive functions. Brain injury, 19(9), 569–583. https://doi.org/10.1080/02699050400013550

88. Ehlhardt, L.A., Sohlberg, M.M., Kennedy, M., Coelho, C., Ylvisaker, M., Turkstra, L., & Yorkston, K. (2008). Evidence-based practice guidelines for instructing individuals with neurogenic memory impairments: what have we learned in the past 20 years? Neuropsychological rehabilitation, 18(3), 300-342. https://doi.org/10.1080/09602010701733190

89. Encyclopædia Britannica, Inc. (n.d.). 3,000 Core Vocabulary Words. The Britannica Dictionary. https://www.britannica.com/dictionary/eb/3000-words

90. Fasotti, L., Kovacs, F., Eling, P.A.T.M., & Brouwer, W.H. (2000). Time pressure management as a compensatory strategy training after closed head injury. Neuropsychological Rehabilitation, 10(1), 47-65. https://doi.org/10.1080/096020100389291

91. Fateh, H.R., Askary-Kachoosangy, R., Shirzad, N., Akbarzadeh-Baghban, A., & Fatehi, F. (2022). The effect of energy conservation strategies on fatigue, function, and quality of life in adults with motor neuron disease: Randomized controlled trial. Current journal of neurology, 21(2), 83–90. https://doi.org/10.18502/cjn.v21i2.10491

92. Fincham, G.W., Strauss, C., & Cavanagh, K. (2023). Effect of breathwork on stress and mental health: A meta-analysis of randomised-controlled trials. Scientific Reports, 13(1), 1-14. https://doi.org/10.1038/s41598-022-27247-y

93. Fleck, C., & Corwin, M. (2013). Evidence-based decisions: Memory intervention for individuals with mild cognitive impairment. EBP Brief, 8, 1-14. https://www.pearsonassessments.com/content/dam/school/global/clinical/us/assets/ebp-briefs/EBPV8A4.pdf

94. Folder, N., Power, E., Rietdijk, R., Christensen, I., Togher, L., & Parker, D. (2024). The Effectiveness and Characteristics of Communication Partner Training Programs for Families of People With Dementia: A Systematic Review. The Gerontologist, 64(4), gnad095. https://doi.org/10.1093/geront/gnad095

95. Franklin, E., & Anjum, F. (2023). Incentive Spirometer and Inspiratory Muscle Training. StatPearls Publishing. https://www.ncbi.nlm.nih.gov/books/NBK572114/

96. Gaddie, A., Kearns, K.P., & Yedor, K. (1991). A Qualitative Analysis of Response Elaboration Training Effects. [Clinical Aphasiology Paper].

97. Gartner-Schmidt, J. (n.d.). Flow Phonation. [Online Course]. Medbridge. https://www.medbridge.com/educate/courses/flow-phonation-jackie-gartner-schmidt

98. Gartner-Schmidt, J., Gherson, S., Hapner, E.R., Muckala, J., Roth, D., Schneider, S., & Gillespie, A.I. (2016). The Development of Conversation Training Therapy: A Concept Paper. Journal of voice : official journal of the Voice Foundation, 30(5), 563-573. https://doi.org/10.1016/j.jvoice.2015.06.007

99. Gillespie, A., & Gartner-Schmidt, J. (n.d.). Conversation Training Therapy [Online course]. Medbridge. https://www.medbridgeeducation.com/courses/details/conversation-training-therapy-jackie-gartner-schmidt-amanda-i-gillespie

100. Gillespie, A.I., Yabes, J., Rosen, C.A., & Gartner-Schmidt, J.L. (2019). Efficacy of Conversation Training Therapy for Patients With Benign Vocal Fold Lesions and Muscle Tension Dysphonia Compared to Historical Matched Control Patients. Journal of speech, language, and hearing research: JSLHR, 62(11), 4062–4079. https://doi.org/10.1044/2019_JSLHR-S-19-0136

101. Gillman, A., Winkler, R., & Taylor, N.F. (2017). Implementing the Free Water Protocol does not Result in Aspiration Pneumonia in Carefully Selected Patients with Dysphagia: A Systematic Review. Dysphagia, 32(3), 345-361. 10.1007/s00455-016-9761-3

102. Gosselink, R., Kovacs, L., Ketelaer, P., Carton, H., & Decramer, M. (2000). Respiratory muscle weakness and respiratory muscle training in severely disabled multiple sclerosis patients. Archives of physical medicine and rehabilitation, 81(6), 747–751. https://doi.org/10.1016/s0003-9993(00)90105-9

103. Greenwood, F. (2020, January). Limb and bulbar onset ALS. ALS Therapy Development Institute. https://www.als.net/news/science-sunday-limb-and-bulbar-onset-als

104. Gupta, S., Yashodharakumar, G.Y., & Vasudha, H.H. (2016). Cognitive behavior therapy and mindfulness training in the treatment of adults who stutter. The International Journal of Indian Psychology, 3(3), 78–87. 10.25215/0303.010

105. Hanson, E.K., Yorkston, K.M., & Britton, D. (2011). Dysarthria in Amyotrophic Lateral Sclerosis: A Systematic Review of Characteristics, Speech Treatment, and Augmentative and Alternative Communication Options. Journal of Medical Speech-Language Pathology, 19(3), 12-30. https://www.ancds.org/assets/docs/EBP/hanson2011.pdf

106. Heape, A. (2018). Modifying the Environment during Mealtime. SpeechPathology.com. https://www.speechpathology.com/ask-the-experts/modifying-the-environment-during-mealtime

107. Haro-Martínez, A., Pérez-Araujo, C. M., Sanchez-Caro, J. M., Fuentes, B., & Díez-Tejedor, E. (2021). Melodic Intonation Therapy for Post-stroke Non-fluent Aphasia: Systematic Review and Meta-Analysis. Frontiers in neurology, 12, 700115. https://doi.org/10.3389/fneur.2021.700115

108. Helm-Estabrooks, N., & Nicholas, M. (2000). Sentence Production Program for Aphasia. Pro-Ed.

109. Helm-Estabrooks, N., Fitzpatrick, P.M., & Barresi, B. (1982). Visual action therapy for global aphasia. The Journal of speech and hearing disorders, 47(4), 385-389. https://doi.org/10.1044/jshd.4704.385

110. Hickey, E.M. (n.d.). Interventions for Persons with Dementia: Creating Supportive Environments [Online Course]. Medbridge. https://www.medbridgeeducation.com/courses/details/interventions-for-persons-with-dementia-creating-supportive-environments

111. Hollo, A., Ensar, B., & Meigh, K.M. (2024). Effects of Script Training to Improve Discourse in a Patient With Chronic Aphasia. Perspective of the ASHA Special Interest Group, 9(1), 35-48. https://doi.org/10.1044/2023_PERSP-23-00161

112. Hopper, T., Mahendra, N., Kim, E., Azuma, T., Azuma, K.A., Azuma, S.J., & Tomoeda, C.E. (2005). Evidence-based practice recommendations for working with individuals with dementia: Spaced-retrieval training. Journal of Medical Speech-Language Pathology, 13(4), xxvii-xxxiv. https://www.ancds.org/assets/docs/EBP/srt_pdf_hooper.pdf

113. Horton, S., Jackson, V., Boyce, J., Franken, C., Siemers, S., John, M.S., Hearps, S., Braden, R., Parker, R., Vogel, A.P., Eising, E., Amor, D.J., Irvine, J., Fisher, S.E., Martin, N.G., Reilly, S., Bahlo, M., Scheffer, I., Morgan, A., & van Reyk, O. (2023). Self-Reported Stuttering Severity Is Accurate: Informing Methods for Large-Scale Data Collection in Stuttering. Journal of Speech, Language, and Hearing Research, 1-10. https://doi.org/10.1044/2023_JSLHR-23-00081

114. Hustad, K.C., & Garcia, J.M. (2005). Aided and unaided speech supplementation strategies: effect of alphabet cues and iconic hand gestures on dysarthric speech. Journal of speech, language, and hearing research, 48(5), 996–1012. https://doi.org/10.1044/1092-4388(2005/068)

115. Hutcheson, K.A., & Lewin, J.S. (2013). Functional assessment and rehabilitation: how to maximize outcomes. Otolaryngologic clinics of North America, 46(4), 657–670. https://doi.org/10.1016/j.otc.2013.04.006

116. Hägglund, P., Olai, L., Ståhlnacke, K., Ståhlnacke, M., Hägg, M., Andersson, M., Koistinen, S., & E, C. (2017). Study protocol for the SOFIA project: Swallowing function, Oral health, and Food Intake in old Age: a descriptive study with a cluster randomized trial. BMC geriatrics, 17(1). https://doi.org/10.1186/s12877-017-0466-8

117. Hwang, N. K., Kim, H. H., Shim, J. M., & Park, J. S. (2019). Tongue stretching exercises improve tongue motility and oromotor function in patients with dysphagia after stroke: A preliminary randomized controlled trial. Archives of oral biology, 108, 104521. https://doi.org/10.1016/j.archoralbio.2019.104521

118. Ingham, R. J., Bothe, A. K., Wang, Y., Purkhiser, K., & New, A. (2012). Phonation interval modification and speech performance quality during fluency-inducing conditions by adults who stutter. Journal of Communication Disorders, 45(3), 198-211. https://doi.org/10.1016/j.jcomdis.2012.01.004

119. Jeon, Y.H., Krein, L., O'Connor, C.M.C., Mowszowski, L., Duffy, S., Seeher, K., & Rauch, A. (2023). A Systematic Review of Quality Dementia Clinical Guidelines for the Development of WHO's Package of Interventions for Rehabilitation. Gerontologist, 63(9), 1536-1555. doi: 10.1093/geront/gnac105. PMID: 36043424; PMCID: PMC10581378.

120. Johansson, B., & Tornmalm, M. (2012). Working memory training for patients with acquired brain injury: effects in daily life. Scandinavian journal of occupational therapy, 19(2), 176–183. https://doi.org/10.3109/11038128.2011.603352

121. Johnson, M.L., Taub, E., Harper, L.H., Wade, J.T., Bowman, M.H., Bishop-McKay, S., Haddad, M.M., Mark, V.W., & Uswatte, G. (2014). An Enhanced Protocol for Constraint-Induced Aphasia Therapy II: A Case Series. American journal of speech-language pathology, 23(1), 60-72. https://doi.org/10.1044/1058-0360(2013/12-0168)

122. Jones, W.E., Benge, J.F., & Scullin, M.K. (2021). Preserving prospective memory in daily life: A systematic review and meta-analysis of mnemonic strategy, cognitive training, external memory aid, and combination interventions. Neuropsychology, 35(1), 123-140. https://doi.org/10.1037/neu0000704

123. Junuzovic-Zunic, L., Sinanovic, O., & Majic, B. (2021). Neurogenic Stuttering: Etiology, Symptomatology, and Treatment. Medical Archives, 75(6), 456-461. https://doi.org/10.5455/medarh.2021.75.456-461

124. Kagan, A., Black, S.E., Duchan, F.J., Simmons-Mackie, N., & Square, P. (2001). Training volunteers as conversation partners using "Supported Conversation for Adults with Aphasia" (SCA): a controlled trial. Journal of speech, language, and hearing research : JSLHR, 44(3), 624–638. https://doi.org/10.1044/1092-4388(2001/051)

125. Kao, Y., Chen, S., Wang, Y., Chu, P., Tan, C., & Chang, W.D. (2017). Efficacy of Voice Therapy for Patients With Early Unilateral Adductor Vocal Fold Paralysis. Journal of Voice, 31(5), 567-575. https://doi.org/10.1016/j.jvoice.2017.04.007

126. Katz, P.O., Dunbar, K.B., Schnoll-Sussman, F.H., Greer, K.B., Yadlapati, R., & Spechler, S.J. (2022). ACG Clinical Guideline for the Diagnosis and Management of Gastroesophageal Reflux Disease. The American journal of gastroenterology, 117(1), 27–56. https://doi.org/10.14309/ajg.0000000000001538.

127. Kaye, R.C., & Cherney, L.R. (2016). Script Templates: A Practical Approach to Script Training in Aphasia. Topics in Language Disorders, 36(2), 136-153. https://doi.org/10.1097/TLD.0000000000000086

128. Kennedy, M.R., & Coelho, C. (2005). Self-regulation after traumatic brain injury: a framework for intervention of memory and problem solving. Seminars in speech and language, 26(4), 242-255. https://doi.org/10.1055/s-2005-922103

129. Khan, A., Podlasek, A., & Somaa, F. (2023). Virtual reality in post-stroke neurorehabilitation - a systematic review and meta-analysis. Topics in stroke rehabilitation, 30(1), 53–72. https://doi.org/10.1080/10749357.2021.1990048

130. Kim, H. D., Choi, J. B., Yoo, S. J., Chang, M. Y., Lee, S. W., & Park, J. S. (2017). Tongue-to-palate resistance training improves tongue strength and oropharyngeal swallowing function in subacute stroke survivors with dysphagia. Journal of Oral Rehabilitation, 44(1), 59-64. 10.1111/joor.12461

131. Kim, J.Y., & Kim, H. (2023). Effects of behavioural swallowing therapy in patients with Parkinson's disease: A systematic review. International journal of speech-language pathology, 25(2), 269–280. https://doi.org/10.1080/17549507.2022.2045356

132. Kleim, J.A., & Jones, T.A. (2008). Principles of experience-dependent neural plasticity: implications for rehabilitation after brain damage. Journal of speech, language, and hearing research, 51(1), S225–S239. https://doi.org/10.1044/1092-4388(2008/018)

133. Knock, T.R., Ballard, K.J., Robin, D.A., & Schmidt, R.A. (2000). Influence of order of stimulus presentation on speech motor learning: A principled approach to treatment for apraxia of speech. Aphasiology, 14(5-6), 653–668. https://doi.org/10.1080/026870300401379

134. Kobak, J. (n.d.). Application of Passy Muir Swallowing and Speaking Valves [Webinar]. Passy Muir.

135. Kotby, N.M., Shiromoto, O., & Hirano, M. (1993). The accent method of voice therapy: Effect of accentuations on F0, SPL, and airflow. Journal of Voice, 7(4), 319-325. https://doi.org/10.1016/S0892-1997(05)80120-1

136. Krekeler, B. N., Rowe, L. M., & Connor, N. P. (2021). Dose in Exercise-Based Dysphagia Therapies: A Scoping Review. Dysphagia, 36(1), 1-32. https://doi.org/10.1007/s00455-020-10104-3

137. Kristensson, J., & Saldert, C. (2018). Naming of Objects and Actions after Treatment with Phonological Components Analysis in Aphasia. Clinical Archives of Communication Disorders. http://dx.doi.org/10.21849/cacd.2018.00367

138. Kurland, J., Stanek, E. J., 3rd, Stokes, P., Li, M., & Andrianopoulos, M. (2016). Intensive Language Action Therapy in Chronic Aphasia: A Randomized Clinical Trial Examining Guidance by Constraint. *American journal of speech-language pathology*, 25(4S), S798–S812. https://doi.org/10.1044/2016_AJSLP-15-0135

139. Lacey, E., Lott, S., Snider, S., Sperling, A., & Friedman, R. (2010). Multiple Oral Re-reading treatment for alexia: The parts may be greater than the whole. Neuropsychological Rehabilitation, 20(4), 601-623. https://doi.org/10.1080/09602011003710993

140. Laiho, A., Elovaara, H., Kaisamatti, K., Luhtalampi, K., Talaskivi, L., Pohja, S., Routamo-Jaatela, K., & Vuorio, E. (2022). Stuttering interventions for children, adolescents, and adults: A systematic review as a part of clinical guidelines. Journal of Communication Disorders, 99, 106242. https://doi.org/10.1016/j.jcomdis.2022.106242

141. Lash & Associates Publishing. (n.d.). Attention process training APT3. Lash & Associates Publishing. Retrieved October, 2024, from https://lapublishing.com/apt3-attention-process-training/

142. Leder, S. B., & Suiter, D. M. (2014). The Yale Swallow Protocol: An Evidence-Based Approach to Decision Making. Springer International Publishing.

143. Leonard, C., Rochon, E., & Laird, L. (2008). Treating naming impairments in aphasia: Findings from a phonological components analysis treatment. Aphasiology, 22(9), 923–947. https://doi.org/10.1080/02687030701831474

144. Leonard, C., Laird, L., Burianová, H., Graham, S., Grady, C., Simic, T., & Rochon, E. (2014). Behavioural and neural changes after a "choice" therapy for naming deficits in aphasia: preliminary findings. *Aphasiology*, 29(4). 506–525. https://doi.org/10.1080/02687038.2014.971099

145. Levine, B., Robertson, I.H., Clare, L., Carter, G., Hong, J., Wilson, B.A., Duncan, J., & Stuss, D.T. (2000). Rehabilitation of executive functioning: an experimental-clinical validation of goal management training. Journal of the International Neuropsychological Society: JINS, 6(3), 299-312. https://doi.org/10.1017/s1355617700633052

146. Levine, B., Schweizer, T.A., O'Connor, C., Turner, G., Gillingham, S., Stuss, D.T., Manly, T., & Robertson, I.H. (2011). Rehabilitation of executive functioning in patients with frontal lobe brain damage with goal management training. Frontiers in human neuroscience, 5(9). https://doi.org/10.3389/fnhum.2011.00009

147. LeWine, H. E. (2023). Gastroesophageal Reflux Disease (GERD). Harvard Health. Retrieved September, 2024, from https://www.health.harvard.edu/a_to_z/gastroesophageal-reflux-disease-gerd-a-to-z

148. Liaw, M. Y., Hsu, C. H., Leong, C. P., Liao, C. Y., Wang, L. Y., Lu, C. H., & Lin, M. C. (2020). Respiratory muscle training in stroke patients with respiratory muscle weakness, dysphagia, and dysarthria – a prospective randomized trial. Medicine (Baltimore), 99(10), e19337. 10.1097/MD.0000000000019337

149. Liu, H., Chen, S., Gao, L., Li, J., Liu, B., Raj, H., Xie, Q., Duan, H., Jiang, Z., Liu, Y., Chen, B., Liu, Y., & Jiang, J. (2022). Comparison Between Combination of Resonant Voice Therapy and Vocal Hygiene Education and Vocal Hygiene Education Only for Female Elementary School Teachers. Journal of voice : official journal of the Voice Foundation, 36(6), 814–822. https://doi.org/10.1016/j.jvoice.2020.09.028

150. Liu, Y., Lee, S.A., & Chen, W. (2022). The Correlation Between Perceptual Ratings and Nasalance Scores in Resonance Disorders: A Systematic Review. Journal of Speech, Language, and Hearing Research, 65(6), 2215–2234. https://doi.org/10.1044/2022_JSLHR-21-00588

151. Livingston, G., Huntley, J., Sommerlad, A., Ames, D., Ballard, C., Banerjee, S., Brayne, C., Burns, A., Cohen-Mansfield, J., Cooper, C., Costafreda, S.G., Dias, A., Fox, N., Gitlin, L.N., Howard, R., Kales, H.C., Kivimäki, M., Larson, E.B., Ogunniyi, A., ... Mukadam, N. (2020). Dementia prevention, intervention, and care: 2020 report of the Lancet Commission. Lancet, 396(10248), 413–446. https://doi.org/10.1016/S0140-6736(20)30367-6

152. Logan, K. J. (2020). Fluency Disorders: Stuttering, Cluttering, and Related Fluency Problems. Plural Publishing, Incorporated.

153. Logemann, J. A. (1986). *Manual for the videofluorographic study of swallowing*. Little, Brown.

154. Lombard, L., & Steinhauer, K. M. (2007). A Novel Treatment for Hypophonic Voice: Twang Therapy. Journal of Voice, 21(3), 294-299. http://dx.doi.org/10.1016/j.jvoice.2005.12.006

155. LSVT Global. (2022). References on LSVT LOUD®, LSVT BIG®, Voice and Speech in Parkinson Disease and Other Neurological Disorders from Ramig and Fox Clinical Research Teams and Other Research Teams. PDF. Retrieved from https://lsvtglobal2016.wpenginepowered.com/wp-content/uploads/2022/09/LSVT-LOUD-and-LSVT-BIG-Reference-List-8_2022.pdf

156. Ludlow, C., Hoit, J., Kent, R., Ramig, L.O., Shrivastav, R., Strand, E., Yorkston, K., & Sapienza, C. (2008). Translating principles of neural plasticity into research on speech motor control recovery and rehabilitation. Journal of speech, language, and hearing research, 51(1), S240–S258. https://doi.org/10.1044/1092-4388(2008/019)

157. Maas, E., Barlow, J., Robin, D., & Shapiro, L. (2002). Treatment of sound errors in aphasia and apraxia of speech: Effects of phonological complexity. Aphasiology, 16(4-6), 609. https://doi.org/10.1080/02687030244000266

158. Maas, E., Robin, D.A., Austermann Hula, S.N., Freedman, S.E., Wulf, G., Ballard, K.J., & Schmidt, R.A. (2008). Principles of Motor Learning in Treatment of Motor Speech Disorders. American Journal of Speech-Language Pathology, 17(3), 277-298. https://doi.org/10.1044/1058-0360

159. Maddy, K., Capilouto, G., & McComas, K. (2014). The effectiveness of semantic feature analysis: An evidence-based systematic review. Annals of Physical and Rehabilitation Medicine, 57(4), 254-267. https://doi.org/10.1016/j.rehab.2014.03.002

160. Mahler, L., & Ramig, L.O. (2012). Intensive treatment of dysarthria secondary to stroke. Clinical Linguistics and Phonetics, 26(8), 681–694. https://doi.org/10.3109/02699206.2012.696173

161. Manning, W., & DiLollo, A. (2017). Clinical Decision Making in Fluency Disorders (4th ed.). Plural Publishing.

162. Mansolillo, A. (n.d.). The Essentials: Dysphagia and Dementia. Medbridge. https://www.medbridge.com/courses/details/essentials-dysphagia-dementia

163. Mansolillo, A. (n.d.). The Essentials: Dysphagia and Head and Neck Cancer [Online course]. Medbridge. https://www.medbridgeeducation.com/courses/details/essentials-dysphagia-head-neck-cancer-angela-mansolillo

164. Mansolillo, A. (n.d.). The Essentials: Dysphagia and Neuromuscular Disease [Online Course]. Medbridge. https://www.medbridge.com/courses/details/essentials-dysphagia-neuromuscular-diseases-angela-mansolillo

165. Mansolillo, A. (n.d.). The Essentials: Dysphagia and Parkinson's Disease [Online course]. Medbridge. https://www.medbridge.com/educate/courses/essentials-dysphagia-parkinsons-disease-angela-mansolillo

166. Mansuri, B., Tohidast, S.A., Soltaninejad, N., Kamali, M., Ghelichi, L., & Azimi, H. (2018). Nonmedical Treatments of Vocal Fold Nodules: A Systematic Review. Journal of voice: official journal of the Voice Foundation, 32(5), 609–620. https://doi.org/10.1016/j.jvoice.2017.08.023

167. Marcotte, K., Laird, L., Bitan, T., Meltzer, J.A., Graham, S.J., Leonard, C., & Rochon, E. (2018). Therapy-Induced Neuroplasticity in Chronic Aphasia After Phonological Component Analysis: A Matter of Intensity. Frontiers in neurology, 9, 225. https://doi.org/10.3389/fneur.2018.00225

168. Marshall, J., Best, W., Cocks, N., Cruice, M., Pring, T., Bulcock, G., Creek, G., Eales, N., Mummery, A.L., Matthews, N., & Caute, A. (2012). Gesture and naming therapy for people with severe aphasia: a group study. Journal of speech, language, and hearing research, 55(3), 726–738. https://doi.org/10.1044/1092-4388(2011/11-0219)

169. Martin-Harris, B., Bonilha, H. S., Brodsky, M. B., Francis, D. O., Fynes, M. M., Martino, R., O'Rourke, A. K., & Rogus-Pulia, N. M. (2021). The Modified Barium Swallow Study for Oropharyngeal Dysphagia: Recommendations From an Interdisciplinary Expert Panel. Perspectives of the ASHA Special Interest Groups, 6(12), 1-10. 10.1044/2021_PERSP-20-00303

170. Martin-Sanchez, C., Calvo-Arenillas, J.I., Barbero-Iglesias, F.J., Fonseca, E., Sanchez-Santos, J.M., & Martin-Nogueras, A.M. (2020). Effects of 12-week inspiratory muscle training with low resistance in patients with multiple sclerosis: A non-randomised, double-blind, controlled trial. Multiple Sclerosis and Related Disorders, 45(102574). https://doi.org/10.1016/j.msard.2020.102574

171. Mauszycki, S.C., & Wambaugh, J. (2020). Acquired Apraxia of Speech: Comparison of Electropalatography Treatment and Sound Production Treatment. American journal of speech-language pathology, 29(1S), 511–529. https://doi.org/10.1044/2019_AJSLP-CAC48-18-0223

172. May, A.A., & Murray, J. (2019). Review of AAC interventions in persons with dementia. International Journal of Language and Communication Disorders, 54(6), 857-874. https://doi.org/10.1111/1460-6984.12491

173. McCarthy, M., Graham Beaumon, J., Thompson, R., & Pringle, H. (2002). The role of imagery in the rehabilitation of neglect in severely disabled brain-injured adults. Archives of Clinical Neuropsychology, 17(5), 407-422. https://doi.org/10.1016/S0887-6177(01)00124-X

174. McCurtin, A., Byrne, H., Collins, L., McInerney, M., Lazenby-Paterson, T., Leslie, P., O'Keeffe, S., O'Toole, C., & Smith, A. (2024). Alterations and Preservations: Practices and Perspectives of Speech-Language Pathologists Regarding the Intervention of Thickened Liquids for Swallowing Problems. *American journal of speech-language pathology*, 33(1), 117–134. https://doi.org/10.1044/2023_AJSLP-23-00226

175. Meerschman, I., D'haeseleer, E., Carty, T., Ruigrok, B., Caleys, S., & Van Lierde, K. (2017). Effect of two isolated vocal facilitating techniques glottal fry and yawn-sigh on the phonation of female speech-language pathology students: A pilot study. Journal of Communication Disorders, 66, 40-50. https://doi.org/10.1016/j.jcomdis.2017.03.004

176. Mehta, R., & Zhu, R. J. (2009). Blue or red? Exploring the effect of color on cognitive task performances. Science, 323(5918), 1226-1229. https://doi.org/10.1126/science.1169144

177. Memorial Sloan Kettering Cancer Center. (2021). Mouth Care During Your Cancer Treatment. Memorial Sloan Kettering Cancer Center. Retrieved September, 2024, from https://www.mskcc.org/cancer-care/patient-education/mouth-care-during-your-treatment

178. Menzies, R., O'Brian, S., Packman, A., Jones, M., Helgadóttir, F.D., & Onslow, M. (2019). Supplementing stuttering treatment with online cognitive behavior therapy: An experimental trial. Journal of communication disorders, 80, 81–91. https://doi.org/10.1016/j.jcomdis.2019.04.003

179. Merriam-Webster, Incorporated. (n.d.). Word Finder: Unscramble Words and Letters. Merriam-Webster. Retrieved October, 2024, from https://www.merriam-webster.com/wordfinder

180. Messing, B.P., Ward, E.C., Lazarus, C.L., Kim, M., Zhou, X., Silinonte, J., Gold, D., Harrer, K., Ulmer, K., Merritt, S., Neuner, G., Levine, M., Blanco, R., Saunders, J., & Califano, J. (2017). Prophylactic Swallow Therapy for Patients with Head and Neck Cancer Undergoing Chemoradiotherapy: A Randomized Trial. Dysphagia, 32(4), 487-500. 10.1007/s00455-017-9790-6

181. Miller, R.G., Jackson, C.E., Kasarskis, E.J., England, J.D., Forshew, D., Johnston, W., Kalra, S., Katz, J.S., Mitsumoto, H., Rosenfeld, J., Shoesmith, C., Strong, M.J., Woolley, S.C., & Quality Standards Subcommittee of the American Academy of Neurology. (2009). Practice parameter update: the care of the patient with amyotrophic lateral sclerosis: drug, nutritional, and respiratory therapies (an evidence-based review): report of the Quality Standards Subcommittee of the American Academy of Neurology. Neurology, 73(15), 1218–1226. https://doi.org/10.1212/WNL.0b013e3181bc0141

182. Miloro, K.V., Pearson, W.G., & Langmore, S.E. (2014). Effortful pitch glide: a potential new exercise evaluated by dynamic MRI. Journal of speech, language, and hearing research : JSLHR, 57(4), 1243–1250. https://doi.org/10.1044/2014_JSLHR-S-13-0168

183. Moore, M., Milosevich, E., Beisteiner, R., Bowen, A., Checketts, M., Demeyere, N., Fordell, H., Godefroy, O., Laczó, J., Rich, T., Williams, L., Woodward-Nutt, K., & Husain, M. (2022). Rapid screening for neglect following stroke: A systematic search and European Academy of Neurology recommendations. European journal of neurology, 29(9), 2596–2606. https://doi.org/10.1111/ene.15381

184. Moore, M.J., Vancleef, K., Riddoch, M.J., Gillebert, C.R., & Demeyere, N. (2021). Recovery of Visuospatial Neglect Subtypes and Relationship to Functional Outcome Six Months After Stroke. Neurorehabilitation and Neural Repair, 35(9), 823-835. https://doi.org/10.1177/15459683211032977

185. Namiki, C., Hara, K., Tohara, H., Kobayashi, K., Chantaramanee, A., Nakagawa, K., Saito, T., Yamaguchi, K., Yoshimi, K., Nakane, A., & Minakuchi, S. (2019). Tongue-pressure resistance training improves tongue and suprahyoid muscle functions simultaneously. Clinical Interventions in Aging, 14, 601-608. https://doi.org/10.2147/CIA.S194808

186. National Foundation of Swallowing Disorders. (2021). Airway Protection Program: Expiratory Muscle Strength Training for Dysphagia Treatment. National Foundation of Swallowing Disorders. Retrieved October, 2024, from https://swallowingdisorderfoundation.com/expiratory-muscle-strength-training/

187. National Institute on Aging. (2022). Falls and Fractures in Older Adults: Causes and Prevention. National Institute on Aging. https://www.nia.nih.gov/health/falls-and-falls-prevention/falls-and-fractures-older-adults-causes-and-prevention

188. National Institute on Aging. (n.d.). Memory, Forgetfulness, and Aging: What's Normal and What's Not? Retrieved 2023, from https://www.nia.nih.gov/health/memory-forgetfulness-and-aging-whats-normal-and-whats-not

189. National Institutes of Health. (2024). What Happens to the Brain in Alzheimer's Disease? National Institute on Aging. Retrieved August, 2024, from https://www.nia.nih.gov/health/alzheimers-causes-and-risk-factors/what-happens-brain-alzheimers-disease

190. National Library of Medicine. (2022, April 17). Communicating with someone with dysarthria. MedlinePlus. Retrieved Feb 9, 2024, from https://medlineplus.gov/ency/patientinstructions/000033.htm

191. National Stuttering Association. (n.d.). National Stuttering Association: Stuttering Support Community. https://westutter.org

192. Netsell, R. (1992). Speech production following traumatic brain injury: Clinical and research implications. Special Interest Divisions: Neurophysiology and Neurogenic Speech and Language Disorders, 2, 1-8.

193. Netsell, R.W. (1995). Speech rehabilitation for individuals with unintelligible speech and dysarthria: The respiratory and velopharyngeal systems. Special Interest Divisions: Neurophysiology and Neurogenic Speech Language Disorders, 5(4), 6-9.

194. Newsome, S.D., Aliotta, P.J., Bainbridge, J., Bennett, S.E., Cutter, G., Fenton, K., Lublin, F., Northrop, D., Rintell, D., Walker, B.D., Weigel, M., Zackowski, K., & Jones, D.E. (2017). A Framework of Care in Multiple Sclerosis, Part 2: Symptomatic Care and Beyond. International journal of MS care, 19(1), 42–56. https://doi.org/10.7224/1537-2073.2016-062

195. Nicola, L., Loo, S.J.Q., Lyon, G., Turknett, J., & Wood, T.R. (2024). Does resistance training in older adults lead to structural brain changes associated with a lower risk of Alzheimer's dementia? A narrative review. Ageing research reviews, 98, 102356. https://doi.org/10.1016/j.arr.2024.102356

196. Niemeier, J. P. (1998). The Lighthouse Strategy: Use of a visual imagery technique to treat visual inattention in stroke patients. Brain Injury, 12(5), 399-406. https://psycnet.apa.org/doi/10.1080/026990598122511

197. Norton, A., Zipse, L., Marchina, S., & Schlaug, G. (2009). Melodic Intonation Therapy: Shared Insights on How it is Done and Why it Might Help. Annals of the New York Academy of Sciences, 1169, 431-436. https://doi.org/10.1111/j.1749-6632.2009.04859.x

198. Novaleski, C.K., Near, L.A., & Benzo, R.P. (2024). Cough: An Introductory Guide for Speech-Language Pathologists. Perspectives of the ASHA Special Interest Groups, 9(1), 75-91. https://doi.org/10.1044/2023_PERSP-23-00203

199. OpenAAC.org. (n.d.). Communication Partner Profile (CPP v1) [PDF]. OpenAAC.org. https://www.openaac.org/assets/cppv1.pdf

200. Oren, S., Willerton, C., & Small, J. (2014). Effects of spaced retrieval training on semantic memory in Alzheimer's disease: a systematic review. Journal of speech, language, and hearing research : JSLHR, 57(1), 247–270. https://doi.org/10.1044/1092-4388(2013/12-0352)

201. O'Brian, C., Carey, B., Hearne, A., Lowe, R., Onslow, M., & Packman, A. (2024). The Camperdown Program Treatment Guide [PDF]. University of Technology Syndey. https://www.uts.edu.au/sites/default/files/2024-07/Camperdown%20Program%20Treatment%20Guide%202024-07-09.pdf

202. Panther, K. (2005). The Frazier Free Water Protocol. Perspectives on Swallowing and Swallowing Disorders (Dysphagia), 14(1), 4-9. https://doi.org/10.1044/sasd14.1.4

203. Park, J. S., Oh, D. H., Chang, M. Y., & Kim, K. M. (2016). Effects of expiratory muscle strength training on oropharyngeal dysphagia in subacute stroke patients: a randomised controlled trial. Journal of Oral Rehabilitation, 43(5), 364-372. 10.1111/joor.12382

204. Park, J., Kim, H., & Oh, D. (2015). Effect of tongue strength training using the Iowa Oral Performance Instrument in stroke patients with dysphagia. Journal of Physical Therapy Science, 27(12), 3631–3634. 10.1589/jpts.27.3631

205. Park, J.S., & Hwang, N.K. (2021). Chin tuck against resistance exercise for dysphagia rehabilitation: A systematic review. Journal of Oral Rehabilitation, 48(8), 968-977. https://doi.org/10.1111/joor.13181

206. Park, S., Theodoros, D., Finch, E., & Cardell, E. (2016). Be Clear: A New Intensive Speech Treatment for Adults With Nonprogressive Dysarthria. American Journal of Speech-Language Pathology, 25(1), 97–110. https://doi.org/10.1044/2015_AJSLP-14-0113

207. Parkinson Voice Project. (n.d.). About SPEAKOUT! Therapy. Parkinson Voice Project. Retrieved June, 2024, from https://parkinsonvoiceproject.org

208. Parkinson Voice Project. (n.d.). Research. Parkinson Voice Project. Retrieved April, 2024, from https://parkinsonvoiceproject.org/education/research/

209. Pedroli, E., Serino, S., Cipresso, P., Pallavicini, F., & Riva, G. (2015). Assessment and rehabilitation of neglect using virtual reality: a systematic review. 9, 226. https://doi.org/10.3389/fnbeh.2015.00226

210. Petersen, R.C., Lopez, O., Armstrong, M.J., Getchius, T.S.D., Ganguli, M., Gloss, D., Gronseth, G.S., Marson, D., Pringsheim, T., Day, G.S., Sager, M., Stevens, J., & Rae-Grant, A. (2018). Practice guideline update summary: Mild cognitive impairment: Report of the Guideline Development, Dissemination, and Implementation Subcommittee of the American Academy of Neurology. Neurology, 90(3), 126–135. https://doi.org/10.1212/WNL.0000000000004826

211. Philippine Academy of Rehabilitation Medicine. (2017). Clinical Practice Guideline on Stroke Rehabilitation (2nd ed.). Philippine Academy of Rehabilitation Medicine. https://parmofficial.com/clinical-practice-guidelines/#flipbook-df_2355/1/

212. Pisegna, J., & Langmore, S. (2018). The Ice Chip Protocol: A Description of the Protocol and Case Reports. Perspectives of the ASHA Special Interest Groups, 3(13), 28. 10.1044/persp3.SIG13.28

213. Pitts, T., Bolser, D., Rosenbek, J., Troche, M., Okun, M.S., & Sapienza, C. (2009). Impact of expiratory muscle strength training on voluntary cough and swallow function in Parkinson disease. Chest, 135(5), 1301-1308. https://doi.org/10.1378/chest.08-1389

214. Plexico, L.W., Manning, W.H., & DiLollo, A. (2005). A phenomenological understanding of successful stuttering management. Journal of Fluency Disorders, 30(1), 1-22. https://doi.org/10.1016/j.jfludis.2004.12.001

215. Plowman, E.K., Tabor-Gray, L., Rosado, K.M., Vasilopoulos, T., Robison, R., Chapin, J.L., Gaziano, J., Vu, T., & Gooch, C. (2019). Impact of expiratory strength training in amyotrophic lateral sclerosis: Results of a randomized, sham-controlled trial. Muscle & nerve, 59(1), 40-46. https://doi.org/10.1002/mus.26292

216. Poirier, S.E., Fossard, M., & Monetta, L. (2021). The efficacy of treatments for sentence production deficits in aphasia: a systematic review. Aphasiology, 37(1), 122-142. DOI: 10.1080/02687038.2021.1983152

217. Popescu, T., Stahl, B., Wiernik, B. M., Haiduk, F., Zemanek, M., Helm, H., Matzinger, T., Beisteiner, R., & Fitch, W. T. (2022). Melodic Intonation Therapy for aphasia: A multi-level meta-analysis of randomized controlled trials and individual participant data. Annals of the New York Academy of Sciences, 1516(1), 76–84. https://doi.org/10.1111/nyas.14848

218. Powell, L.E., Glang, A., Ettel, D., Todis, B., Sohlberg, M.M., & Albin, R. (2012). Systematic instruction for individuals with acquired brain injury: results of a randomised controlled trial. Neuropsychological rehabilitation, 22(1), 85–112. https://doi.org/10.1080/09602011.2011.640466

219. Purdy, M., Coppens, P., Brookshire Madden, E., Mozeiko, J., Patterson, J., Wallace, S.E., & Freed, D. (2018). Reading comprehension treatment in aphasia: a systematic review. Aphasiology, 33(6), 629-651. 10.1080/02687038.2018.1482405

220. Raymer, A.M., McHose, B., Smith, K.G., Iman, L., Ambrose, A., & Casselton, C. (2012). Contrasting effects of errorless naming treatment and gestural facilitation for word retrieval in aphasia. Neuropsychological rehabilitation, 22(2), 235-266. https://doi.org/10.1080/09602011.2011.618306

221. Raymer, A. M., & Roitsch, J. (2023). Effectiveness of Constraint-Induced Language Therapy for Aphasia: Evidence From Systematic Reviews and Meta-Analyses. American journal of speech-language pathology, 32(5S), 2393–2401. https://doi.org/10.1044/2022_AJSLP-22-00248

222. Reid Health. (n.d.). Parkinson Voice Project. Reid Health. Retrieved January 2025, from https://www.reidhealth.org/parkinson-voice-project

223. Rener, V. (2020, February 11). Strength training can help protect the brain from degeneration. The University of Sydney. https://www.sydney.edu.au/news-opinion/news/2020/02/11/strength-training-can-help-protect-the-brain-from-degeneration.html

224. Richardson, B. (n.d.). Foundations of Respiratory Muscle Training: Dysphagia Therapy. Medbridge. Retrieved January, 2023, from https://www.medbridge.com/courses/details/foundations-of-respiratory-muscle-training-dysphagia-therapy-brooke-richardson

225. Robbins, J., Butler, S.G., Daniels, S.K., Diez Gross, R., Langmore, S., Lazarus, C.L., Martin-Harris, B., McCabe, D., Musson, N., & Rosenbek, J. (2008). Swallowing and dysphagia rehabilitation: translating principles of neural

plasticity into clinically oriented evidence. Journal of speech, language, and hearing research, 51(1), S276–S300. https://doi.org/10.1044/1092-4388(2008/021)

226. Robbins, J., Kays, S. A., Gangnon, R. E., Hind, J. A., Hewitt, A. L., Gentry, L. R., & Taylor, A. J. (2007). The effects of lingual exercise in stroke patients with dysphagia. Archives of Physical Medicine and Rehabilitation, 88(2), 150-158. 10.1016/j.apmr.2006.11.002

227. Roberts, C. (2020, October). How to Choose a Medical Alert System. Consumer Reports. Retrieved August, 2024, from How to Choose a Medical Alert System

228. Robison, R., Tabor-Gray, L.C., Wymer, J.P., & Plowman, E.K. (2018). Combined respiratory training in an individual with C9orf72 amyotrophic lateral sclerosis. Annals of clinical and translational neurology, 5(9), 1134–1138. https://doi.org/10.1002/acn3.623

229. Rodrigues, D.S., de Souza, P.T.D.R., Orsi, J.S.R., Souza, P.H.C., & Azevedo-Alanis, L.R. (2023). Oral care to reduce costs and increase clinical effectiveness in preventing nosocomial pneumonia: A systematic review. The journal of evidence-based dental practice, 23(2), 101834. https://doi.org/10.1016/j.jebdp.2023.101834

230. Rodríguez, M.A., Crespo, I., Del Valle, M., & Olmedillas, H. (2020). Should respiratory muscle training be part of the treatment of Parkinson's disease? A systematic review of randomized controlled trials. Clinical rehabilitation, 34(4), 429–437. https://doi.org/10.1177/0269215519896054

231. Rose, T. A., Worrall, L., & McKenna, K. (2003). The effectiveness of aphasia-friendly principles for printed health education materials for people with aphasia following stroke. Aphasiology, 17(10), 947–963. https://doi.org/10.1080/02687030344000319

232. Rose, T.A., Worrall, L.E., Hickson, L.M., & Hoffman, T.C. (2011). Aphasia friendly written health information: Content and design characteristics. International Journal of Speech-Language Pathology, 13(4), 335–347. https://doi.org/10.3109/17549507.2011.560396

233. Rosenbek, J., Lemme, M., Ahern, M., Harris, N., & Wertz, T. (1973). A treatment for apraxia of speech in adults. Journal of Speech and Hearing Disorders, 38(4), 462–472. https://doi.org/10.1044/jshd.3804.462

234. Rosenberg, M.D. (2014). Using Semi-Occluded Vocal Tract Exercises in Voice Therapy: The Clinician's Primer. Perspectives on Voice and Voice Disorders, 24(2), 71-79. https://doi.org/19407505002400020071

235. Saban, K.L., Tell, D., & De La Pena, P. (2022). Nursing Implications of Mindfulness-Informed Interventions for Stroke Survivors and Their Families. Stroke, 53(11), 3485–3493. https://doi.org/10.1161/STROKEAHA.122.038457

236. Sapienza, C., & Hoffman, B. (2020). Voice disorders. Plural Publishing, Incorporated.

237. Sataloff, R.T. (2018). Treatment of Voice Disorders (2nd ed.). Plural Publishing, Inc.

238. Scullin, M.K., Jones, W.E., Phenis, R., Beevers, S., Rosen, S., Dinh, K., Kiselica, A., Keefe, F.J., & Benge, J.F. (2022). Using Smartphone Technology to Improve Prospective Memory Functioning: A Randomized Controlled Trial. Journal of the American Geriatrics Society, 70(2), 459-469. https://doi.org/10.1111/jgs.17551

239. Segura, T., Medrano, I.H., Collazo, S., Maté, C., Sguera, C., Casero, H., Salcedo, I., & Taberna, M. (2023). Symptoms timeline and outcomes in amyotrophic lateral sclerosis using artificial intelligence. Scientific Reports, 13(1), 1-10. https://doi.org/10.1038/s41598-023-27863-2

240. Sherrell, Z. (2020). GERD Diet: Foods to avoid, what to eat, and plans for acid reflux. MedicalNewsToday. Retrieved October, 2024, from https://www.medicalnewstoday.com/articles/314690#foods-to-avoid

241. Shin, S., Park, H., & Hill, K. (2021). Identifying the Core Vocabulary for Adults With Complex Communication Needs From the British National Corpus by Analyzing Grouped Frequency Distributions. Journal of speech, language, and hearing research : JSLHR, 64(11), 4329–4343. https://doi.org/10.1044/2021_JSLHR-21-00211

242. Silverman, E.P., Miller, S., Zhang, Y., Hoffman-Ruddy, B., Yeager, J., & Daly, J.J. (2017). Effects of expiratory muscle strength training on maximal respiratory pressure and swallow-related quality of life in individuals with multiple sclerosis. Multiple Sclerosis Journal – Experimental, Translational and Clinical, 3(2). https://doi.org/10.1177/2055217317710829

243. Simmons-Mackie, N., Raymer, A., & Cherney, L.R. (2016). Communication Partner Training in Aphasia: An Updated Systematic Review. Archives of physical medicine and rehabilitation, 97(12), 2202–2221.e8. https://doi.org/10.1016/j.apmr.2016.03.023

244. Singh, S. (2023). Visual Neglect. EyeWiki by The American Academy of Opthamology. https://eyewiki.aao.org/Visual_Neglect

245. Sisskin, V., & Baer, M. (2016). Treb: éliminer la lutte contre le bégaiment. Ortho Magazine (Elsevier), 22(123), 14-17.

246. Smania, N., Bazoli, F., Piva, D., & Guidetti, G. (1997). Visuomotor imagery and rehabilitation of neglect. Archives of Physical Medicine and Rehabilitation, 78(4), 430-436. https://doi.org/10.1016/S0003-9993(97)90237-9

247. Smania, N., Bazoli, F., Piva, D., & Guidetti, G. (1997). Visuomotor imagery and rehabilitation of neglect. Archives of physical medicine and rehabilitation, 78(4), 430–436. https://doi.org/10.1016/s0003-9993(97)90237-9

248. Sohlberg, M. M., & Mateer, C. A. (2001). Cognitive Rehabilitation: An Integrative Neuropsychological Approach (M. M. Sohlberg & C. A. Mateer, Eds.; 2nd ed.). Guilford Publications.

249. Sohlberg, M.M., & Mateer, C.A. (1989). The assessment of cognitive communicative functions in head injury. Topics in Language Disorders, 9(2), 15–33. https://doi.org/10.1097/00011363-198903000-00004

250. Sohlberg, M.M., Kennedy, M., Avery, J., Coelho, C., Turkstra, L., Ylvisaker, M., & Yorkston, K. (2007). Evidence-based practice for the use of external aids as a memory compensation technique. Journal of Medical Speech-Language Pathology, 15(1), x–li.

251. Sparks, R., Helm, N., & Albert, M. (1974). Aphasia rehabilitation resulting from melodic intonation therapy. Cortex, 10(4), 303–316. https://doi.org/10.1016/S0010-9452(74)80024-9

252. Sparks, R., & Holland, A. (1976). Method: Melodic intonation therapy for aphasia. Journal of Speech and Hearing Disorders, 41(3), 287–297. https://doi.org/10.1044/jshd.4103.287

253. Stamenova, V., & Levine, B. (2019). Effectiveness of goal management training® in improving executive functions: A meta-analysis. Neuropsychological rehabilitation, 29(10), 1569–1599. https://doi.org/10.1080/09602011.2018.1438294

254. Steffy, E. A., Stans, S.E.A., Dalmesman, R.J.P., de Witte, L.P., Smeets, H.W.H., & Beurskens, A.J. (2017). The role of the physical environment in conversations between people who are communication vulnerable and health-care professionals: a scoping review. Disability and Rehabilitation, 39(25), 2594-2605. 10.1080/09638288.2016.1239769

255. Stemple, J. (n.d.). Vocal Function Exercises. Online Course. https://www.medbridgeeducation.com/courses/details/vocal-function-exercises-joseph-stemple-speech-langauge-pathology-vocal-therapy

256. Stemple, J.A. (n.d.). Resonant Voice Therapy: Generalizing the Balanced Voice [Online course]. Medbridge. https://www.medbridge.com/course-catalog/details/resonant-voice-therapy-generalizing-the-balanced-voice-joseph-stemple-speech-langauge-pathology

257. Stemple, J.A., Roy, N., & Klaben, B.K. (2018). Clinical voice pathology: Theory and management (6th ed.). Plural Publings, Incorporated.

258. Stevens, E.R., & Glaser, L.E. (1983). Multiple Input Phoneme Therapy: An Approach to Severe Apraxia and Expressive Aphasia. [Clinical Aphasiology Paper]

259. Strand, E.A., Duffy, J.R., Clark, H.M., & Josephs, K. (2014). The Apraxia of Speech Rating Scale: a tool for diagnosis and description of apraxia of speech. Journal of communication disorders, 51, 43-50. https://doi.org/10.1016/j.jcomdis.2014.06.008

260. Sullivan, L., Martin, E., & Allison, K. M. (2024). Effects of SPEAK OUT! & LOUD Crowd on Functional Speech Measures in Parkinson's Disease. American journal of speech-language pathology, 33(4), 1930–1951. https://doi.org/10.1044/2024_AJSLP-23-00321

261. Swiderski, A. M., Quique, Y. M., Dickey, M. W., & Hula, W. D. (2021). Treatment of Underlying Forms: A Bayesian Meta-Analysis of the Effects of Treatment and Person-Related Variables on Treatment Response. https://doi.org/23814764000300140072

262. Swiech, P., Sullivan, A., & Helfrich, C. (2021). Self-Feeding With the Adult Population: Back to Basics. American Occupational Therapy Association. American Occupational Therapy Association.

263. Sze, W.P., Hameau, S., Warren, J., & Best, W. (2020). Identifying the components of a successful spoken naming therapy: a meta-analysis of word-finding interventions for adults with aphasia. Aphasiology, 35(1), 33–72. https://doi.org/10.1080/02687038.2020.1781419

264. Tabor, L., Plowman, M., & Martin, K. (2017). Living with ALS: Adjusting to Swallowing Changes and Nutritional Management in ALS. The ALS Association. https://www.als.org/sites/default/files/2020-04/lwals_08_2017.pdf

265. Taub, E. (2012). The Behavior-Analytic Origins of Constraint-Induced Movement Therapy: An Example of Behavioral Neurorehabilitation. The Behavior Analyst, 35(2), 155-178. https://doi.org/10.1007/BF03392276

266. The Center on Budget and Policy Priorities. (n.d.). Goal Plan Do Review/Revise. Gpdd.org. Retrieved Sept, 2022, from https://www.gpdrr.org

267. Tennant, K., Long, A., & Toney-Butler, T. J. (2023). Active Listening. In StatPearls. StatPearls Publishing.Varkey B. (2021). Principles of Clinical Ethics and Their Application to Practice. Medical principles and practice : international journal of the Kuwait University, Health Science Centre, 30(1), 17–28. https://doi.org/10.1159/000509119

268. The Stuttering Foundation. (2013). A Fresh Look at Avoidance Reduction Therapy. Stuttering Foundation. Retrieved October, 2024, from https://www.stutteringhelp.org/content/fresh-look-avoidance-reduction-therapy

269. Theis, S.M., & Carlson, A. (2022). Voice Therapy. International Journal of Head and Neck Surgery, 13(1), 27-31. https://doi.org/10.5005/jp-journals-10001-1518

270. Thompson, C. (2001). Language Intervention Strategies in Aphasia and Related Neurogenic Communication Disorders (R. Chapey, Ed.; 4th ed.). Lippincott Williams & Wilkins.

271. Thompson, C., & Chapey, R. (2001). Treatment of Underlying Forms: A linguistic Specific Approach for Sentence Production Deficits in Agrammatic Aphasia (4th ed., Vol. pp. 605-628). Lippincott Williams & Wilkins.

272. Thompson, C.K., & Shapiro, L.P. (2005). Treating agrammatic aphasia within a linguistic framework: Treatment of Underlying Forms. Aphasiology, 19(10-11), 1021–1036. https://doi.org/10.1080/02687030544000227

273. Togher, L., Douglas, J., Turkstra, L.S., Welch-West, P., Janzen, S., Harnett, A., Kennedy, M., Kua, A., Patsakos, E., Ponsford, J., Teasell, R., Bayley, M.T., & Wiseman-Hakes, C. (2023). INCOG 2.0 Guidelines for Cognitive Rehabilitation Following Traumatic Brain Injury, Part IV: Cognitive-Communication and Social Cognition Disorders. Journal of Head Trauma Rehabilitation, 38(1), 65-82. 10.1097/HTR.0000000000000835

274. Tomik, B., & Guiloff, R.J. (2010). Dysarthria in amyotrophic lateral sclerosis: A review. Amyotrophic lateral sclerosis : official publication of the World Federation of Neurology Research Group on Motor Neuron Diseases, 11(1-2), 4-15. https://doi.org/10.3109/17482960802379004

275. Troche, M.S., Okun, M.S., Rosenbek, J.C., Musson, N., Fernandez, H.H., Rodriguez, R., Romrell, J., Pitts, T., Wheeler-Hegland, K.M., & Sapienza, C.M. (2010). Aspiration and swallowing in Parkinson disease and rehabilitation with EMST: a randomized trial. Neurology, 75(21), 1912–1919. https://doi.org/10.1212/WNL.0b013e3181fef115

276. U.S. Centers for Disease Control and Prevention. (2024, May 9). Facts About Falls | Older Adult Fall Prevention. CDC. https://www.cdc.gov/falls/data-research/facts-stats/index.html

277. University of Michigan Medicine. (2019, September). Resonant Placement: Exercises for Vocal Therapy [Video]. Michigan Medicine Patient Education. https://careguides-videos.med.umich.edu/media/t/1_5i8unqa4

278. van Hees, S., Angwin, A., McMahon, K., & Copland, D. (2013). A comparison of semantic feature analysis and phonological components analysis for the treatment of naming impairments in aphasia. Neuropsychological rehabilitation, 23(1), 102-132. https://doi.org/10.1080/09602011.2012.726201

279. Van Riper, C. (1973). The Treatment of Stuttering. Prentice-Hall.

280. Verdolini Abbott, K., Li, N.Y., Branski, R.C., Rosen, C.A., Grillo, E., Steinhauer, K., & Hebda, P.A. (2012). Vocal exercise may attenuate acute vocal fold inflammation. Journal of voice : official journal of the Voice Foundation, 26(6), 814.e1–814.e13. https://doi.org/10.1016/j.jvoice.2012.03.008

281. Verdolini-Marston, K., Burke, M.K., Lessac, A., Glaze, L., & Caldwell, E. (1995). Preliminary study of two methods of treatment for laryngeal nodules. Journal of Voice, 9(1), 74-85. https://doi.org/10.1016/S0892-1997(05)80225-5

282. Vertigan, A.E., Theodoros, D.G., Gibson, P.G., & Winkworth, A.L. (2006). Efficacy of speech pathology management for chronic cough: A randomised placebo controlled trial of treatment efficacy. Thorax, 61(12), 1065-1069. https://doi.org/10.1136/thx.2006.064337

283. Wambaugh, J. (n.d.). Treatment of Acquired Apraxia of Speech: Therapeutic Approaches and Practice Guidelines. Medbridge. https://www.medbridge.com/course-catalog/details/treatment-of-acquired-apraxia-of-speech-therapeutic-approaches-and-practice-guidelines

284. Wambaugh, J.L., & Mauszycki, S.C. (2010). Sound production treatment: Application with severe apraxia of speech. Aphasiology, 24(6-8), 814–825. https://doi.org/10.1080/02687030903422494

285. Wambaugh, J.L., Kalinyak-Fliszar, M.M., West, J.E., & Doyle, P.J. (1998). Effects of treatment for sound errors in apraxia of speech and aphasia. Journal of Speech, Language, and Hearing Research, 41(4), 725–743. https://doi.org/10.1044/jslhr.4104.725

286. Wambaugh, J.L., Kallhoff, L., & Nessler, C. (2021). Sound Production Treatment for Acquired Apraxia of Speech: An Examination of Dosage in Relation to Probe Performance. American journal of speech-language pathology,, 30(1S), 425–440. https://doi.org/10.1044/2020_AJSLP-19-00110

287. Wambaugh, J.L., Nessler, C., & Wright, S. (2013). Modified Response Elaboration Training: Application to Procedural Discourse and Personal Recounts. American journal of speech-language pathology, 22(2), S409–S425. https://doi.org/10.1044/1058-0360(2013/12-0063)

288. Wambaugh, J.L., Nessler, C., Cameron, R., & Mauszycki, S.C. (2013). Treatment for Acquired Apraxia of Speech: Examination of Treatment Intensity and Practice Schedule. American Journal of Speech-Language Pathology, 22(1), 84-102. https://doi.org/10.1058036000220001084

289. Wambaugh, J.L., Nessler, C., Wright, S., & Mauszycki, S.C. (2014). Sound production treatment: effects of blocked and random practice. American journal of speech-language pathology, 23(2), S225–S245. https://doi.org/10.1044/2014_AJSLP-13-0072

290. Wang, Y.T., Kent, R.D., Duffy, J.R., & Thomas, J.E. (2005). Dysarthria associated with traumatic brain injury: speaking rate and emphatic stress. Journal of communication disorders, 38(3), 231-260. https://doi.org/10.1016/j.jcomdis.2004.12.001

291. Wang, Z., Wang, Z., Fang, Q., Li, H., Zhang, L., & Liu, X. (2019). Effect of Expiratory Muscle Strength Training on Swallowing and Cough Functions in Patients With Neurological Diseases: A Meta-analysis. American journal of physical medicine & rehabilitation, 98(12), 1060–1066. https://doi.org/10.1097/PHM.0000000000001242

292. Wang, Z., Wu, L., Fang, Q., Shen, M., Zhang, L., & Liu, X. (2019). Effects of capsaicin on swallowing function in stroke patients with dysphagia: A randomized controlled trial. Journal of Stroke and Cerebrovascular Diseases, 23(6), 1744-1751. https://doi.org/10.1016/j.jstrokecerebrovasdis.2019.02.008

293. Watando, A., Ebihara, S., Ebihara, T., Okazaki, T., Takahashi, H., Asada, M., & Sasaki, H. (2004). Daily oral care and cough reflex sensitivity in elderly nursing home patients. Chest, 126(4), 1066–1070. https://doi.org/10.1378/chest.126.4.1066

294. Watts C. R. (2016). A retrospective study of long-term treatment outcomes for reduced vocal intensity in hypokinetic dysarthria. BMC ear, nose, and throat disorders, 16, 2. https://doi.org/10.1186/s12901-016-0022-8

295. Watts, C.R., & Awan, S.N. (2019). Laryngeal Function and Voice Disorders Basic Science to Clinical Practice (1st ed.). Thiem.

296. Watts, C.R., Diviney, S.S., Hamilton, A., Toles, L., Childs, L., & Mau, T. (2015). The effect of stretch-and-flow voice therapy on measures of vocal function and handicap. Journal of voice : official journal of the Voice Foundation, 29(2), 191–199. https://doi.org/10.1016/j.jvoice.2014.05.008

297. Watts, C.R., Hamilton, A., Toles, L., Childs, L., & Mau, T. (2019). Intervention Outcomes of Two Treatments for Muscle Tension Dysphonia: A Randomized Controlled Trial. Journal of speech, language, and hearing research, 62(2), 272–282. https://doi.org/10.1044/2018_JSLHR-S-18-0118

298. Weightman, M., Vining Radomski, M., Mashima, P., & Roth, C. (2015). Mild Traumatic Brain Injury Rehabilitation Toolkit. Borden Institute. https://medcoe.army.mil/borden-tb-tbi

299. Werden Abrams, S., Gandhi, P., & Namasivayam-MacDonald, A. (2023). The Adverse Effects and Events of Thickened Liquid Use in Adults: A Systematic Review. American Journal of Speech-Language Pathology, 32(5), 2331-2350. https://doi.org/10.1044/2023_AJSLP-22-00380

300. Whelan, B. M., Theodoros, D., Cahill, L., Vaezipour, A., Vogel, A. P., Finch, E., Farrell, A., & Cardell, E. (2022). Feasibility of a Telerehabilitation Adaptation of the Be Clear Speech Treatment Program for Non-Progressive Dysarthria. Brain sciences, 12(2), 197. https://doi.org/10.3390/brainsci12020197

301. Winiker, K., & Kertscher, B. (2023). Behavioural interventions for swallowing in subjects with Parkinson's disease: A mixed methods systematic review. International Journal of Language & Communication Disorders, 58(4), 1375-1404. https://doi.org/10.1111/1460-6984.12865

302. Winkens, I., van Heugten, C.M., Wade, D., & Fasotti, L. (2009). Training patients in Time Pressure Management, a cognitive strategy for mental slowness. Clinical Rehabilitation, 23(1), 79-90. https://doi.org/10.1177/0269215508097855

303. Witkowski, D., & Baker, B. (2012). Addressing the content vocabulary with core: Theory and practice for nonliterate or emerging literate students. Perspectives on Augmentative and Alternative Communication, 21(3), 74–81. https://doi.org/10.1044/aac21.3.74

304. Yang, S., Park, J.W., Min, K., Lee, Y.S., Song, Y.J., Choi, S.H., Kim, D.Y., Lee, S.H., Yang, H.S., Cha, W., Kim, J.W., Oh, B.M., Seo, H.G., Kim, M.W., Woo, H.S., Park, S.J., Jee, S., Oh, J.S., Park, K.D., ... Choi, K.H. (2023). Clinical Practice Guidelines for Oropharyngeal Dysphagia. Annals of rehabilitation medicine, 47(Suppl 1), S1-S26. https://doi.org/10.5535/arm.23069

The Adult Speech Therapy Protocols Pack

305. Yiu, E.M., Lo, M.C., & Barrett, E.A. (2017). A systematic review of resonant voice therapy. International Journal of speech-language pathology, 19(1), 17–29. https://doi.org/10.1080/17549507.2016.1226953

306. Youmans, G., Youmans, S.R., & Hancock, A.B. (2011). Script Training Treatment for Adults With Apraxia of Speech. American Journal of Speech-Language Pathology, 20(1), 23-37. https://doi.org/10.1044/1058-0360(2010/09-0085)

307. Young, A., & Spinner, A. (2023). Velopharyngeal Insufficiency. StatPearls Publishing.

308. Zhang, X., Li, J., & Du, Y. (2022). Melodic Intonation Therapy on Non-fluent Aphasia After Stroke: A Systematic Review and Analysis on Clinical Trials. Frontiers in Neuroscience, 15, 753356. https://doi.org/10.3389/fnins.2021.753356

309. Zumbansen, A., & Tremblay, P. (2019). Music-based interventions for aphasia could act through a motor-speech mechanism: A systematic review and case–control analysis of published individual participant data. Aphasiology, 33(4), 466–497. https://doi.org/10.1080/02687038.2018.1506089

310. Zumbansen, A., Peretz, I., & Hébert, S. (2014). Melodic intonation therapy: Back to basics for future research. Frontiers in Neurology, 5, 1-11. https://doi.org/10.3389/fneur.2014.00007

About the Author

Chung Hwa Brewer is a speech-language pathologist, university instructor, and author. She is the co-founder of Adult Speech Therapy, a company with the mission to help clinicians feel confident in their jobs.